The Humility

D1414493

The Humility of God

by John Macquarrie

THE WESTMINSTER PRESS
Philadelphia

© John Macquarrie 1978

First edition
Published by The Westminster Press ®
Philadelphia, Pennsylvania

PRINTED IN THE UNITED STATES OF AMERICA

9 8 7 6 5 4 3 2 1

Library of Congress Cataloging in Publication Data

Macquarrie, John.
  The humility of God.

  1. Meditations. I. Title.
  BV4832.2.M233   242   77-18707
  ISBN 0-664-24200-6

CONTENTS

PREFACE

The meditations which follow touch on only some of the many aspects of Christian faith and life, but there runs through them all a theme which, I think, needs emphasizing in our time – the humility of God, his down-to-earthness, his involvement in the life of his creatures.

Most of the meditations had their origins as addresses given in the course of my duties as Canon of Christ Church Cathedral, Oxford. I wish to express my indebtedness to the Cathedral and to all who contribute in so many different ways to its life, which in a unique manner combines worship, beauty and scholarship.

Christk Church JOHN MACQUARRIE
Oxford

I

THE SHARING

The title of this collection of meditations, *The Humility of God*, will probably remind some readers of the rather similar title of a small book by Karl Barth, *The Humanity of God*. This is no accident, for humility and humanity are closely related. The old Latin grammarians believed that the words *humilitas* and *humanitas* were both derived from *humus*, the earth. The humble remain close to the ground, while human beings, it was believed, have bodies that were formed from the earth. So whether we think of the humility of God or of the humanity of God, we are focusing attention on his earthliness. This is a necessary corrective in our thinking about God, for our minds seem to dwell more naturally on his heavenliness. But he is God of earth as well as God of heaven. He is called the Most High, but he has been pleased to make himself known as the Most Low.

We begin by reflecting on the act of creation. In conferring the gift of existence on others than himself, God limited himself and took upon himself a commitment which already opens the way that leads to the incarnation and the passion.

Creation

'Why is there something rather than just nothing?' That question was put by the philosopher Leibniz. It seems a very odd question, yet it is one that many of us find ourselves asking, though we may put it in different words. For, when we think of it, it is surely a very strange fact that we exist and are capable of thinking, and that there exists a world that seems to have brought us forth. Where do we come from, and where does the world come from? Is there a reason for the world's existence, any purpose or meaning to it? Or is it just there, so to speak?

Some people would say that it is idle to ask such questions, for there is no way of answering them. But the questions do not go away. We have what Eric Mascall calls 'the capacity for contemplative wondering', and this capacity for wonder is one of the most precious things in human life. If men had not yielded to the lure of wondering, they would never have advanced any distance along the road of knowledge. Even when we come to the end of what can be known, that is to say, demonstrated by reason and experience, we still keep wondering. Then we throw out probes beyond knowledge, probes into the unknown, the probes that we call faith or belief. Of course, this is not just a leap in the dark. Belief takes account of all the evidence available.

Religious faith answers the questions about a reason for the existence of the world by saying that God has created it. 'In the beginning, God created the heavens and the earth' (Gen. 1.1).

But does this really tell us anything, or shed any light on the riddle of existence? For what do we know about God? Or what meaning can we attach to the word 'created'?

I think we can say that we have at least the beginning of an answer. There is already sufficient content in the claim that God created the heaven and the earth to differentiate it from another claim, the one which seems to be its chief rival. That is the claim that the world and all in it, including ourselves, have come into being simply by chance. 'Our number came up in the Monte Carlo game' was how the French scientist, Jacques Monod, expressed this point of view. When we say that God created the world, we are denying that other point of view. We are affirming that we are not here by chance, and that there is some sense and meaning at work in the way things are. The difference between these two ways of understanding our own origins also makes it clear why people will go on wondering about the question, even if agnostics and positivists tell them that the question should not be asked. They will go on asking because this is no mere academic question, but one that has profound consequences for the practical business of living. If we can believe that there is some intelligence, purpose and meaning in the scheme of things, then to that extent we can feel at home in the world and have some hope for its future and for the future of mankind. But if man's appearance is accidental – and some have even considered it a regrettable accident – then we must always be haunted by a sense of alienation, and in so bleak a situation it would seem that only the most conscientious of persons could seriously engage themselves.

Let us explore further what can be meant by saying, 'In the beginning God created the heavens and the earth.' Let us begin on a low key, and for the present try to exclude from our minds the full Christian conception of God. Let us take the word 'God' in a minimal sense, to mean a reality that is intelligent and purposeful, but without going on at this stage to hold that he is also 'pure unbounded love'. Then we can see that there are some features of the universe that do seem to point to its origin in an intelligent and purposeful source of being. The universe seems to be a highly orderly affair, built up of a limited number of basic types of particles which have the capacity for combining in innumerable complex patterns. Furthermore, it is a universe that has itself brought forth beings having intelligence and purpose. On the other hand, one has also to say that the picture is ambiguous. As well as order, there is randomness, and what seemed at one time to be purpose may also be explained in naturalistic ways. There seems no way in which one could conclusively reckon up this balance sheet. But we can say at least that the claim that God (understood still in a fairly minimal way) is the author of the world is not an absurd idea. It presents an intelligible alternative to the atheistic view, and it has some *prima facie* evidence in its favour. So it is certainly legitimate to explore the meaning of belief in a Creator God further, especially since it has such important practical consequences and affects our whole 'feel' for our own existence in the world.

Now let us think somewhat more deeply on the meaning of the word 'created'. It is significant that both in the original Hebrew and in the English translations of the Bible, a special verb is used to express the relation of God to the world. It is not said simply that God 'made' the world, but that he 'created' the world. When I simply 'make' something, that which I make is quite external to myself, and often I have no further interest in it. This is especially true in the modern world. In factories, people make things or even only parts of things with the aid of machinery. They may never even see the finished objects, and their relation to them is quite transitory. On the other hand, if I 'create' something, this word indicates a much more intimate relationship. We normally use this verb for an artist, and we customarily talk of the 'creativity' of the artist. When

3

an artist paints a picture, for instance, this is not something merely external to himself, or something to which he bears only a casual and passing relationship. He has, in a true sense, put himself into his creation. The relation is, we could say, one of *caring*. Once the picture has been made, it has of course become an object on its own. Though it began in the imagination of the artist, it has now been externalized, and stands over against him. Yet, in another equally true sense, that picture is an extension of the artist himself. He is now in the picture, just as the picture has been in him. There is a sense too in which he has committed himself and even pledged himself in painting the picture. He acknowledges it as his own – and this point is only reinforced by the fact that artists sometimes disown their compositions – and he is responsible for it.

The analogy of the artist helps us to understand better what is meant when it is said that God created the world. His act of creation was not an arbitrary exercise of sovereign power, nor was the world which he created something entirely external to him and left to go its own way. Rather, we must say, as in the case of the human artist, this was a caring act. God gave a measure of independent reality to that which had hitherto existed only in his thought. This means that to some extent he already was putting himself into his creation; or, to put the matter in another way, his creation was also a self-emptying. At the same time, by giving to the creation a measure of independence, God was also limiting himself. This point is seen especially when we remember that the creation had the potentiality for bringing forth finite spiritual creatures like ourselves, possessed of a freedom which we can pit against God. 'Man,' said Herder, 'is God's risk.'

So when we begin to analyse the idea of creation, we find that it is not so much an exercise of power as rather an exercise of love and generosity, an act of self-limitation and even of self-humiliation on the part of God. His love and generosity lead him to share existence with his creatures. He puts himself into the creation. He commits himself to it and takes responsibility for it, though at the same time he commits a share of the responsibility to the creatures. And in all this there is inevitably not just a limitation of power but also God's making himself vulnerable, for there cannot be this love and sharing and conferring of freedom without the possibility of suffering on the part of him who loves and shares and confers. Although we say that God did this 'in the beginning', that is only our mythological way of saying what we believe to be God's nature from eternity. He has

4

always been creative love, and it is love rather than power that is his primary attribute.

From our consideration of the meaning of creation, we have been able to perceive a much richer content in the word 'God' than we did at the beginning of our meditation. The God who creates is not just some vague Supreme Intelligence or anything of the sort. He is the God who is always coming out from himself in love and sharing and self-giving, and the commitment that he makes to his creation already points forward to the fuller involvement of the incarnation and passion.

Original Sin and Original Righteousness

In the Old Testament, the story of creation is followed by the story of the fall. God, it was believed, had brought forth a creation that was 'very good'; but clearly the world that we see around us is not very good, though perhaps it is not very bad either. The story of the fall was meant to account for the obvious imperfection of the created world. Man had used his freedom to disobey God, and so evil had come into the world.

Of course, the doctrine of a fall of man does not imply that there must once have been a golden age. It means rather that from its first appearance on earth, the human race has never fulfilled the possibilities open to it but has constantly fallen away from them. Perhaps this was inevitable, and is the price that has to be paid for a universe in which there are finite centres of freedom. There is the risk or even the near certainty that these many centres will not choose to be in harmony either with God or with each other. Even before the fall, to speak mythologically, there was a built-in instability in the world. This was complicated further by the ambiguity of man's relation to inanimate nature. So far as this could be understood as outside of God and other than God, it was available for man's use, and indeed man had the duty to share in shaping the world and making it his home. He was explicitly commanded to subdue the earth. Yet to the extent that the world is the object of God's caring, it deserves respect. The creation calls for understanding and appreciation as well as for exploitation, and it is not easy to know how to keep these attitudes in balance. In modern times especially, we have become aware how man and nature have got out of step, and how man's greedy exploitation of natural resources is reacting to his own detriment in many ways.

5

An open creation, capable of advance and development, is bound to be characterized by an instability. It is potentiality rather than something already finished, and sin seems unavoidable. It was Reinhold Niebuhr who said paradoxically that sin is not necessary, but it is inevitable. He meant that it is not an inexorable fate imposed upon the human race; yet the very fact that in creation God set something other than himself in a situation of relative autonomy outside of himself made a conflict unavoidable.

In his day Niebuhr shocked liberal progressive America by reviving not only the idea of sin but that of original sin. To talk of original sin is to recognize that there is a kind of solidarity of the human race in sin. Sin is corporate as well as individual. There are distorted social structures, wrong value systems, unjust priorities, the oppression of some human groups by others, and many other evils that, however they may have originated, pervade humanity as a whole. They not only cover humanity in its geographical spread, but they also maintain themselves from generation to generation. Each new individual only learns to become a person through taking his place in society, and so it follows that he inevitably is affected by the sinful distortions of that society and may well reinforce them himself.

All this sounds very much like fate. It may remind us of the view of the ancient Israelites that the sins of the fathers are visited on the children and on the children's children, so that they are all caught in the grip of a crushing destiny. If this were to be the fate of creation, then it might have been better if creation had never taken place.

But some of the clearsighted Hebrew prophets broke out of such a fatalistic view of sin. Ezekiel, for instance, thought that such teaching was an affront to God. He himself taught a bold individualism. Every single person, he maintained, has a responsibility for his own life and is not bound by the past. He will be judged according to his deeds. If he turns away from the wickedness of the previous generation, he will not suffer for their sins, while on the other hand, if he does evil himself, he cannot expect to take refuge in any merits that may have belonged to his forebears.

This teaching brought hope into what would otherwise be a very depressing situation. For if the future were nothing but the working out of the past, if there were no possibilities of radically new departures in human life, if everything has already been decreed and settled by an inexorable fate, then what would be the point in striving or aspiring after anything better than we know? What would be the point in continuing the experiment of God's creation?

We still have our fatalists at the present day. Some believe that the world is swept along by vast social, political, economic, technological and biological forces which we can neither understand nor control. Others tell us that we are not even masters in our own house, so to speak, and that our very beliefs are not the result of rational judgment but of sociological pressure and psychological influences. It cannot be denied that there is some truth in all this, just as there is truth in a doctrine of original sin. Technology, for instance, has acquired a life of its own, so that it is hard to know whether man is now developing his technology or whether his technology is forcing him into paths which he would not have chosen. But if this fatalistic view of the situation were the whole truth, it would be a sad state of affairs. Fatalistic doctrines are paralysing and are bound to have an inhibiting effect both on action and judgment.

But in theological and philosophical questions, the truth rarely lies all on one side. Surely those prophets who stressed the responsibility of new individuals and new generations were right in not leaving to fatalism the last word, and in human history there have been many instances of surprising renewals and reinvigorations. But here we have to avoid exaggeration on the other side. It is true that we are never completely trapped by fate, so that we could only passively endure the consequences of what had been decided in the past. Yet it is equally true that we never face completely open horizons where everything is possible. What is open to us at any given time is to some extent conditioned and limited by what has gone before. Just as there are fatalists who would stifle us with the doctrine that nothing can be changed, so there are equally mistaken people (and there seem to be many such enthusiasts in the Christian church today) who talk irresponsibly of the 'open future' and seem to suggest that we can simply shrug off the past and begin everything *de novo*. They do considerable damage in encouraging utopian and unrealistic expectations.

The truth of the human situation is the more complicated one that new possibilities are indeed open to each individual and to each generation, but they occur in the context of a history which already limits what can be open, and sometimes does so very severely. In other words, although original sin is not an iron fate utterly depriving the human race of freedom and the possibility of new departures, it is a reality with which we have to reckon, and it hangs like a pall over the human scene. That great rationalist, Immanuel Kant, writing at the very height of the Enlightenment, began his book *Religion within the Limits of Reason Alone* with a chapter on 'The Radical Evil in Human Nature'. That gives his book a realism which was not common at a time when even the best minds were filled with optimism and ideas of unlimited progress. One may contrast with Kant's sober realism the unbounded optimism of another great Enlightenment figure, Lessing: 'It will come! It will assuredly come! the time of the perfecting, when man, the more convinced his understanding feels about an even better future . . . will do right because it is right.'[1] Looking back over the two hundred years of history since Lessing wrote these words, we can see how badly he failed to take account of original sin, the radical evil in human nature.

It has been said that from the point of view of Christian faith, there are only two basic heresies about man. One holds that he is so bad and so sunk in sin that salvation has become impossible for him. The other holds that he is so naturally good that salvation is unnecessary for him. But we must not allow ourselves to be driven either into a despairing pessimism or into a facile optimism.

If the doctrine of original sin is not to have the last word, it must be confronted with a doctrine of original righteousness. After all, in the Old Testament story righteousness is more original than sin, for man and woman were made in the image of God before they fell into sin. If we reject the heresy that the human race is utterly evil and corrupted, then we have to acknowledge that deeper than the perversion of sin is this original drive towards righteousness. So long as man is recognizably human, he retains something of the image of God as his true potentiality, and even to the extent that he feels uneasy and dissatisfied with his life, he is reaching out for something better. If we have all had experience of human sinfulness, all of us too have had experience of human goodness. Sometimes that goodness may have met us in quite unexpected places, and when we have had such experiences of native goodness, we have felt our faith both in human nature and in God restored.

But is this all that we can say? Are we left with a wholly ambiguous picture, in which original sin and original righteousness strive together for the possession of the soul of man? A picture in which the victory certainly does not go wholly to sin, yet it does not go to righteousness either, for the drive towards the good is never quite able to throw off the pull of sin and seems to struggle free only in isolated acts?

Perhaps that is all we could say if God has simply created things in the beginning and left them to take their course. But if creation means that God committed himself to his world and, in a sense, put himself into it, then this also means that man is not alone in his struggles. Sin is opposed not only by man's enfeebled original righteousness, but by grace, which has never been absent. By 'grace' we do not mean some magical power of God forcibly intervening in the events of history or in the inner life of man. We mean rather a humble presence. Grace is God's presence and solidarity with his creatures in their strivings. God is not a distant figure presiding in the skies, but one who stands with his creation, to strengthen and encourage whatever is affirmative in it. In the Old Testament, this solidarity of God with his creatures was expressed in terms of the 'covenants' that he made with them. He made his covenant with Noah and the whole creation, he made his covenant with Abraham and his descendants, he made a covenant with Moses and the emergent nation of Israel. The Hebrew prophets looked forward to a new and still deeper covenant that God would make with his people, and Christians, looking back, have seen in this a pointer to the new covenant in Christ.

Original sin is a fact that we would be very foolish to leave out of our reckoning. Original righteousness too is a fact, and as it is more original than sin, it points to the true destiny of man. But the picture remains an ambiguous one until we recognize also God's grace, his strengthening and encouraging presence as he stands in solidarity with his creatures even in the lowest depths of the creation.

Hope

It is very typical of the Bible that the depressing story of the fall of man is relieved by a gleam of hope. God says to the serpent: 'I will put enmity between you and the woman, and between your seed and her seed; he shall bruise your head and you shall bruise his heel' (Gen. 3.15). This is the so-called *Protevangelium*, the first announcement of the gospel, because from an early time Christian theologians read into this verse a promise that from the seed of the woman there would arise a Saviour who would overcome evil and set the human race upon a new path.

9

Hope is found as widely as humanity itself. We human beings live in time, and we need both memory and hope. Without these, we could have no identity as persons, or as communities. We need a history that makes us who we are, but equally we need a future that will let us become what there is still in us to become. To be denied either a past or a future is a dehumanizing experience. To be denied a past, as has happened to those who were transported from their homeland as slaves, is to be made rootless, anonymous, without the dignity of a tradition and a place in the human family. To be denied a future, either through fear or deprivation of opportunity, is to be denied the possibility of attaining one's full human stature, and so to be reduced to hopelessness and despair.

Like many of the other qualities that are essential to personal being, hope is not easy to define. Perhaps we could say that it is like an open space in front of a person. Into that space he can project his dreams and aspirations. That space gives him room for manoeuvre and growth, so that he can develop his potentialities. Into that space he projects himself, the self that he is called by God to become. Without such a space, personal development is stunted and arrested.

As long as people accept the challenge and responsibility of life, they have hope. Their work, their study, their family life are all lived in hope, and they constantly commit themselves to the future and look for a fulfilment in the future. Hope must have very deep roots in our humanity, for over and over again we find to our surprise that people whom we expected to be overwhelmed by disasters and disappointments and made a prey to despair, are in fact still projecting their lives into the future and still striving forward in quiet hope. So it has been from the beginning, for although the shadow of evil and death has fallen over every life, it has been met by hope and belief in a promise of better things.

What are the grounds of hope? I believe that hope is one of several features of human life which, if we reflect on it in depth, points finally to God as its ultimate ground. There is scarcely an adequate ground for hope in the natural world alone. It it true that in nature decay is usually followed by renewal, but renewal in its turn is followed by further decay, as in the familiar cycle of the seasons. Nietzsche expressed the pessimistic depth of his philosophy by the idea of eternal recurrence – the belief that things return always to the same place from which they began. On this naturalistic view of reality, as finite and contingent through and through, there can never be anything new. There is never any radical break in the cycle, only a reshuffling of the elements that go to make up universal history. Even the theory of evolution does not alter this situation, for evolution in one part of the universe may be accompanied by devolution in another, and whatever is built up through evolution seems destined in the long run to break down again.

For the roots of hope, we have to look beyond the natural order, and we find them ultimately only in God. We remember St Augustine's famous words: 'Thou hast made us towards thyself!' Man is created not to move in a circle, trapped in eternal recurrence, but to move out beyond himself towards God. Modern philosophers talk about man's transcendence, ancient theologians talked more specifically of his deification. Hope is intimately linked with this innate drive in man to go out beyond himself – to go out in the direction of God, whose image is already within him and seeking realization. Man's calling and destiny is to bring to ever fuller realization the divine image in human life. Thus moral theologians have seen hope not primarily as an emotion or a state of mind, but as a virtue, and furthermore they have seen it as not just a natural virtue but – along with faith and love – as one of the three so-called 'theological' virtues. It is interesting to note that several atheistic philosophers have agreed about the essentially religious character of hope. According to Feuerbach, 'hope is faith in relation to the future'. In our own time, the neo-Marxist thinker Ernst Bloch has declared that 'where there is hope, there is religion'.

That hope is grounded in religion seems certainly to be the biblical teaching on the subject. We have seen that God's promise brought a glimmer of hope into the story of the fall. As we go on to consider the history of Israel, we find it to be in many respects a history of disasters. There must have seemed little or nothing in the world on which Israel could base any hope. But again and again they found a new future opening before them – a future which they believed to be given by God and which was a fulfilment of his ancient promises, though a fulfilment that transcended their expectations. At the time when the fortunes of Israel seemed to be at their lowest ebb, hope burned most brightly and assumed a new form – the hope of the end of the age and the consummation of God's purpose. The new eschatological form of religion that had emerged was one of the critical moments in the history of religion, and was destined to be of the highest significance for Christianity.

The hope of Israel lives on to this day, in spite of the terrible sufferings that have attended the Jewish people in those centuries that have passed since the time of the sufferings recorded in the Old Testament and Apocrypha. The Jewish theologian and philosopher, Abraham Heschel, recalls the grim days of the Nazi terror when the Jewish people of Europe were being systematically exterminated in Auschwitz and the other death camps, and when every door of escape seemed closed to them. 'What should have been our answer to Auschwitz?' he asks. Should the answer have been to give up hope and to give up once for all belief in the God who was supposed to have been guiding his people for so long to a promised land? No. Heschel answers his question with a counter-question: 'Is the state of Israel God's humble answer to Auschwitz?' Whatever one may think of Near Eastern politics and of the rival claims of Jews and Arabs, it would be hard not to be impressed by the hope which the new state of Israel inspired in those Jews who survived the attempted genocide of the Hitler epoch. The sanctuary of Israel, by providing a new home and a new future for a multitude of men, women and children who had been near to perishing, has become for them a symbol of hope. It has provided that open space, which we saw to belong to the essence of hope.

It is important for Christians to be aware that Israel's hope did not end with the Old Testament. It is important for us too to be aware that other peoples, including the Palestinian Arabs, have their legitimate hopes. Although some of these hopes may seem to exclude one another, the history of hope has been such that we should be learning the lesson that hopes are sometimes fulfilled in ways that had not been anticipated and that if charity and justice prevail, the legitimate hopes of all people can be realized.

Christian hope, of course, centres on Jesus Christ. He is the one who, in Christian belief, fulfilled the prophecy and bruised the serpent's head. Yet it may seem just as strange to find hope in Christ as to find it in the chequered history of Israel. If we confine ourselves to the plain historical record, it is that of a man whose message was rejected, whose love and service were spurned, who was condemned as a criminal and subjected to a cruel death. What ground can be seen in this for hope?

Yet the experience of the Christian community was that out of these grim happenings God did indeed open a new way forward. Crucifixion and rejection led through atonement and resurrection to a new life – and however we may understand some of these ideas, they were realities in the lives of those who experienced them. God again made himself known as a God of hope, even in a very dark hour, and inspired his people to build again for the future.

Hope, of course, contains no guarantee. It does not make things easy, but gives strength to undertake the difficult. It is very important indeed to notice that there is a great difference between hope and optimism. Hope is humble, trustful, vulnerable. Optimism is arrogant, brash, complacent. Hope has known the pang of suffering and has perhaps even felt the chill of despair. The word hope should not be lightly spoken by people who have never had any cause for despair. Only one who has cried *de profundis* can really appreciate the meaning of hope. By contrast, optimism has not faced the enormity of evil or the results of the fall of man and the disfiguring sin that affects all human life, both personal and social. What drives some people to atheism is not a genuinely biblical hope but the spectacle of an insensitive optimism, masquerading as such hope. When one seriously considers such dreadful events as Auschwitz or the rejection of Christ, optimism appears as blasphemous. It would be a better response to conclude that the world and human life are an absurdity. For how could such things happen, save in an absurd and godless world?

Hope is not optimism; it is nothing so superficial as the easy belief that all is going to turn out well in the end. But equally, hope saves us from pessimism, the acceptance that the universe is a sorry scheme of things without final meaning. Hope is rather the faith that when man falls and even when the worst evils happen in this ambiguous world, we never find ourselves at the end of the road. The creator God is ahead of us, waiting to open a new possibility. To be sure, it then becomes our responsibility to seize on that possibility and bring it to realization. God opens the way, but it is left to us whether we shall go along the way that is opened. There is no automatic progress, for God has given to man the awesome responsibility of sharing with him in the shaping of the world. Our hope is not that *in spite of* everything we do, all will turn out for the best. Our hope is rather that God is with us and ahead of us, opening a way in which we can responsibly follow.

Calling

The theme of God's standing with his people and sharing with them the adventures of history finds expression in a whole series of incidents in the Bible, in which God calls men and women to some task or mission. The pattern of calling, hearing and responding recurs again and again. God does not govern the world from outside or by arbitrary decree. He seeks the service and co-operation of men and women, and makes them his agents. Again, his activity in the world is not just of a general or abstract kind. He calls particular men and women and works through particular situations. According to the Bible, he chose a particular people to attain to the knowledge of himself, and within that people he chose particular individuals to be leaders and interpreters. Some people have difficulty with this 'scandal of particularity', as it has sometimes been called. But history is compounded of the universal and the particular, and it seems to be in particular individuals that the decisive initiatives are taken.

Abraham is the first great figure to receive the divine call. He is summoned to turn his back on the settled life of the affluent cities of Mesopotamia, and to go out into the unformed wilderness to build up there a new nation. At a later time, Moses was called to go down into Egypt and to undertake the apparently impossible task of liberating the tribes and leading them out to a new life. Many other heroes and prophets of Israel received their calls. These calls came in various ways. With Abraham, the call seems to have been some inner constraint. With Moses, it was a vision of a burning bush and the hearing of a voice. With Isaiah, it was a vision in the Temple. Sometimes the person receiving the call was moved at first to resist it, for such a call upsets the whole pattern of life and leads into ways that are unknown and that may well be filled with suffering.

How can we try to understand this calling of God? Were these men and women not just deluding themselves when they supposed that God was calling them? When, how, where does God speak to us? How could we ever be sure that it is God who is calling, and that we are not just deceiving ourselves into thinking that our own prejudices are in fact God's will?

Some people would brush away all these stories about the calling of God, and would say it is just so much superstition. God, if indeed there is a God, does not speak to men or call them. There do seem to be times when God is silent, and perhaps our time is one of them.

14

God seems to be absent. But there have been times like this in the past too. The story of how Samuel heard God calling him in the sanctuary at Shiloh begins by saying that 'the word of the Lord was rare in those days' (I Sam. 3.1). But even at any time, there is an elusiveness about the voice of God. It is a still small voice, even a humble voice, not a loud and strident one.

Because the voice of God is a quiet and elusive one, we do right to be hesitant when either we ourselves or others think that the voice has been heard. We must be suspicious of those who are too forward in claiming to know what God is saying to our times or what he is doing in the world today. Churchmen and, even more, statesmen, who claim to be familiar with the counsels of God and with his plan of action in the world, are a dangerous breed. In these matters, a measure of reticence and even agnosticism is always in order.

And the reason for counselling this caution is, that when God speaks, there must always be a measure of ambiguity. His communication is not direct, but indirect. He does not speak to us with an unmistakable, audible voice, as our friends do. When Samuel heard the voice in the sanctuary, he thought at first that it was the old priest Eli who was calling him. Three times he ran to the old man and said, 'You called me!' After the third time, Eli said, 'No, it must be God.'

Was God's voice then different from Eli's voice? Was it not through Eli's teaching that Samuel had learned about God, so that in a very real sense God had called him through Eli? When he heard God's voice, it sounded just like Eli's voice, just as when Bernadette saw the vision of the Blessed Virgin, she looked just like the statue in the local church. These things could not happen any other way. We hear God's voice in and through human voices. He speaks to us through them, and in turn he is calling us so that he may work through us.

Does that mean then that we can explain Samuel's experience, by saying that as he learned more of God through Eli's teaching, he became more and more aware of the contradiction between a God of righteousness and the evils that flourished in Eli's household? And that perhaps at first through his loyalty and affection towards Eli, he had tried to suppress these disturbing thoughts and put them out of his mind? But that now at last the truth finally forced itself on his consciousness, and made him recognize that what he had learned to call the word of God was now speaking not through Eli but against him – or, better, both through him and against him?

Yet, when we have said this, have we really 'explained' anything at all? We have simply recognized that God's call or God's word are never experienced in their bare form, whatever that would be, but always mediated through the creatures – in practice, usually in a human word. God communicates indirectly. We hear his voice in and through a human voice or a human experience of some sort. That means too that it is perceived only by faith, and is never perceived in the way we perceive some empirical phenomenon.

Why then do we say it is the voice *of God*? Is not this supposed perception of faith a mere superstition? Is it not enough to recognize a human voice, a human conscience, a human experience? Why bring God into it?

We say that this is God who is calling in order to express the ultimacy of such moments. I call these moments 'ultimate' because in them persons are addressed in the very depth of their being, at a level that seems to lie beyond that of our everyday experiences. It is a matter of life and death, of the making or breaking of the person addressed, a question of to be or not to be. To be sure, it is my heart, my conscience, my neighbour that speaks. Yet in and through and with that human address there can be heard the note of ultimacy, the claim of the holy, and we know that here we have to deal with that which is most real, most binding, most compelling – in brief, with the mystery of God.

As we think of all those callings in the history of Israel, we see how they build up and form a coherent pattern, so that we can say that through them God is calling the human race to the destiny he has prepared for it. Yet this universal call has its origin in highly particular calls – calls directed to individuals who were usually very obscure persons but who through their calling became men and women of destiny. We can understand what Paul meant when he wrote to the Christians of Corinth: 'Consider your call, brethren; not many of you were wise according to worldly standards, not many were powerful, not many were of noble birth; but God chose what is foolish in the world to shame the wise, God chose what is weak in the world to shame the strong, God chose what is low and despised in the world, even things that are not, to bring to nothing things that are, so that no human being might boast in the presence of God' (I Cor. 1.26–29). The humility of God is seen not least in the fact that he sought the co-operation of these obscure individuals to give voice to his universal call – the scandal of particularity, indeed!

The call came at last to an obscure maiden of Nazareth. This time, according to the tradition, it came in the form of an angelic vision. The spark of original righteousness that had been preserved and nursed in Israel was ready to burst into flame. The common grace that had never failed had done its work of sanctification. The successive callings had brought Israel in the person of Mary to a new level of responsiveness. It was the fullness of the time, when mankind was ready to receive the gift of God's presence in a new way. And the response was not lacking: 'Be it unto me according to thy word' (Luke 1.38).

But although God bestowed his presence in a new way through Jesus Christ, whom we call the incarnate Lord, this was also a confirmation that he continues to speak through the human reality. The elusive voice of God which men and women had heard fitfully and ambiguously in the voice of the neighbour or the voice of conscience or in visions or in some other way has found a new and fuller expression in a human life, the life of Jesus Christ the living word of God.

Of course, the ambiguity is still not wholly removed, and it never can be in our earthly existence where God's self-communication is of necessity indirect and mediated. Many people saw and heard Jesus Christ, but were far from believing that he came from God. Even those who were waiting for a word from God had their doubts. 'Can any good thing come out of Nazareth?' (John 1.46). Surely, if God were going to speak a word, especially a word that would sum up and universalize the many fragmentary callings of the past, he would not choose an obscure man from Nazareth, an obscure town in an obscure province. Yet this is how God always had uttered his call, using the foolish, the weak, the low and despised, to confound the wise and the powerful. If some saw in Jesus only another prophet or rabbi, there were others who found in him an ultimacy that they found nowhere else. I have used the word 'ultimate' to designate that which we meet in human experience, yet that which has a depth stretching beyond our grasp and speaking to us of what is finally real and binding, the holy mystery that we call God. The life of Jesus Christ was a life lived in this world, as you and I have to live, but a life in which we meet ultimate freedom, ultimate creativity, ultimate love, ultimate moral authority, so that with the first disciples we confess that in him we have beheld the glory of the Father.

Jesus Christ is the word made flesh, and it is in and through him

17

that we hear most clearly the voice of God calling us. That voice has never been silent. It was calling men and women in the ages before Christ, and is still calling today. But now as then, the voice does not call in any dramatic, shattering way, but quietly, hidden in and with the human realities of daily life. Modern life is so hurried and frequently so superficial that one can easily miss the overtones of God's calling. But his voice is still addressing and summoning us.

2

THE COMING

God was never an absentee God, dwelling apart from his creation. From the beginning, he has been deeply involved with his creation. His Spirit has been bringing forth new possibilities and healing the wounds which sin has inflicted. God's commitment to the creation has been an ever deepening commitment, and Christians believe that with Jesus Christ that commitment took on a new dimension in what we call the incarnation. God's presence and activity, which had always been in the world, were concentrated and focused in a human life which manifested on the finite level what is most central in the life of God himself.

Revolution

The fact that we date our era from the birth of Jesus Christ is so familiar to us that we never give the matter a thought. But I think we may be bold to say that the coming of Jesus Christ was indeed a turning-point in the history of this planet. His coming brought the shift of the ages, the crisis of judgment, the moment of truth. It is true that in some ways the coming of Christ was a fulfilment of longings and expectations, and continuous with man's earlier experience of God. Yet here was something so startlingly new that it went beyond and even contradicted many of the expectations. The long familiar world and its ways were brought into question, the established order was shaken and there took place the true transvaluation of all values. Yet since it was a new righteousness that appeared, there was not only a judgment of the existing order but the promise of a world radically renewed and transformed.

It would not be inappropriate to apply to the coming of Christ the concept of revolution, for the pattern of events which we discern in that coming is very close to the one seen in the phenomenon that we call revolution. It is not surprising that down the ages the most radical Christians have been men of an apocalyptic turn of mind, men who looked for the end of the age in which they were living and for a new age in which life would be transformed. Some of the enthusiasts of the Middle Ages, such as Joachim of Fiore, were like that. So at the time of the Reformation were radicals like Thomas Münzer, who took the side of the peasants while Luther allied himself with the princes. It is not surprising either that some secular and even anti-Christian revolutionaries have been attracted by those elements in Christian teaching which speak of the shift of the ages and the creation of a new heaven and a new earth. It is therefore worthwhile to investigate more closely the relation between the coming of Christ and revolution.

There is, of course, an obvious ambiguity in the word 'revolution'. It may mean going round in a complete circle so that you come back to the place from which you began. We say of a rapidly turning wheel, for instance, that it completes so many revolutions per second. In ancient times, many people supposed that history itself had a cyclic character, so that good times and bad times would keep coming round, rather like the seasons of the year. Shortly before the birth of Christ, the Roman poet Virgil in his famous fourth Eclogue sang of the new age beginning in Rome: 'The last age is coming. From the fullness of the times is being born a great new order.' Virgil probably understood this as the return of a Golden Age, though Christians later applied his words to the coming of Christ. Nowadays we would understand revolution differently, not as the return of a Golden Age with the circling of the heavens, but as the inbreaking of the radically new and unprecedented. But such an understanding of revolution was not possible in pre-Christian times, and it is the advent of Jesus Christ that above all gives substance to the belief that there can come about a radical renewal, transfiguration and transvaluation.

Still, the ambiguity is not abolished, between revolution as the return of the cycle, and revolution as the emergence of the new. Let us call them respectively Revolution A and Revolution B. The tragedy of history has been that Revolution B, the renewal and transfiguration of life, has continued to be haunted by Revolution A, moving round in a circle to the starting point, so that very few revolutions have fulfilled their promises, and most of them have lapsed back into forms of oppression scarcely distinguishable from those that they set out to break.

It is a strange accident that one of the most revolutionary books ever written – in the sense of Revolution B, the emergence of the genuinely new – contained in its title the word 'revolution' used in the sense of Revolution A, going round in a circle. I mean the work of Copernicus, father of modern astronomy who revolutionized our conception of the universe. His book was called *De Revolutionibus Orbium Coelestium,* 'Concerning the Revolutions of the Heavenly Bodies'. When we look back now, we speak of the 'Copernican revolution', and contrast the new Copernican age with all the ages that had gone before. Perhaps there never has been a greater intellectual revolution, and its consequences have reached far beyond the borders of astronomy and even of the sciences into every province of life. When Luther heard of Copernicus' teaching, he declared: 'The fool would turn the world upside down!' Luther was mistaken in regarding Copernicus as a fool, but he was one of the first to grasp the revolutionary significance of his teaching. Things could never be the same again, perhaps not even in theology. For the seed of a suspicion had been sown, a suspicion that was to grow in the following centuries, that the human race, now dethroned from the centre of the universe, may not after all be the darling of a divine Creator but just an insignificant incidental phenomenon in the incomprehensibly vast ocean of space and time.

It is worth dwelling a little longer on the Copernican revolution, for it helps us to grasp more clearly the nature of Revolution B. Some years ago Thomas Kuhn wrote an influential book entitled *The Structure of Scientific Revolutions.*[2] His thesis was that normal scientific work goes on within the framework of a paradigm or model which serves to guide research. As time goes on, anomalies accumulate. At first scientists can take care of these by modifying the paradigm or model in one respect or another, but there comes a time when the pressures on the old framework have become so great that a crisis comes about and there is a revolutionary shift in paradigms. Thus, in astronomy the old Ptolemaic model of the universe had to be modified and remodified by adding new planetary epicycles to account for the observed motions of the heavenly bodies, but eventually the critical point was reached when the old model was falling apart under the strains and was more and more ceasing to be credible, so that the time was ripe for that drastic shift of models we call the Copernican revolution.

Although I have chosen the example of a scientific or intellectual revolution, a similar pattern can be discerned in political and social revolutions. Corresponding to the drive for intellectual clarity in scientific revolutions, there is at work in the political revolution what Hannah Arendt has called 'the passion for humanization'. That passion may be partially satisfied in a society by a series of modifications to its structures and by the removal of its more obvious injustices and irritations. But a time comes when such piecemeal reforms can no longer stand up to the pressures, and the existing order is seen to be incapable of adjusting itself to the new level of demands and expectations. That is the moment of revolution, when the old structures irretrievably break down; there is a radical reshuffling of powers and institutions, and a new order emerges.

These brief remarks on the phenomenon of revolution, as we find it in the secular areas of science and politics, can help us better to understand the spiritual revolution that occurred with the new coming of God, the advent of Jesus Christ. They help us to understand the expression, 'the fullness of the times'. They teach us that history consists not only in the steady passage of time but in moments of concentrated weight. There are times when events quietly unfold themselves in causal sequence, but there are also creative moments of crisis when pressures that have been long building up shatter the stable shape of things, so that there is a change in the direction of events and an inbreaking of the new. It is precisely those moments of crisis that may afford a deeper insight into what is going on in the whole process.

That is why Christian theologians have never been willing to go along with rationalist and idealist philosophers who have sought to turn Christian teaching into a set of eternal truths. Theologians have, on the contrary, insisted on the particularity and concreteness of certain events, especially the event of Jesus Christ. That event is in one sense a fulfilment of what has gone before, and in continuity with it; but equally it is judgment, discontinuity and the emergence of the new. Lessing claimed that 'accidental truths of history can never serve as the basis for eternal truths of reason', but it would be much more adequate to say that living truth comes to light in the blending and sometimes the clash of the particular and the universal, the temporal and the timeless.

I have used the expression 'spiritual revolution' to describe the advent of Jesus Christ. What do I mean by this? The expression is used to describe a type of revolution that is different from both scientific and political revolutions and yet resembles them in structure. But can we fill in the content more clearly?

It has been fashionable in recent years to depict Jesus Christ as a revolutionary, but a revolutionary of the conventional political kind, dedicated to the violent overthrow of government. Apart from the historical implausibility of such a view, it is a far too superficial reading of the revolutionary role of Christ in history. The revolutionary whose horizon is limited to the political and who relies on violence and even escalates violence may indeed begin with 'the passion for humanization' but he almost inevitably ends in dehumanization. He slips back from Revolution B to Revolution A, for he gets locked in the circle of violence and substitutes new oppressions for the old ones.

The passion for humanization needs something much more profound for its fulfilment. It needs what I have called 'spiritual revolution'. This would mean a deep shift in human nature itself, with new motives, new goals, new methods, even new concepts of God taking the place of those that had dominated the scene thitherto. It was a neo-Marxist philosopher, Herbert Marcuse, who declared that changes in social structures and political institutions are not enough and that what we need is 'a new type of man, with new needs, capable of finding a qualitatively different way of life'. But to demand this kind of change takes us from politics into religion. With Jesus Christ, something radically new did come into the world. A new creation took place and a new humanity was born. This was the transvaluation of values, with love and meekness set above power. This was the shift of paradigms, when the proud and lofty gods of the ancient world, yes, even the God of Israel to the extent that he had been misconceived in terms of power, gave way to the suffering crucified Lord. This was the revolutionary crisis, when the old order was judged and found wanting, and the new age dawned. The fulfilment of the new age still lies far ahead, but a hope has been born and a revolution has commenced, and these cannot be annulled.

Incarnation

One of the profoundest passages in all literature is the prologue to St John's gospel. It makes two great assertions. The first is a timeless or eternal truth: 'In the beginning was the Word, and the Word was with God, and the Word was God' (John 1.1). The second is a particular or historical truth: 'And the Word became flesh and dwelt among us, full of grace and truth; we have beheld his glory, glory as of the only Son from the Father' (John 1.14).

The first of these truths, the one that we have called timeless or eternal, is taught in one form or another by all the religions and religious philosophies. It asserts that this universe is not just a product of chance but has some rationale to it. The Greek term, Logos, translated in the Bible as the Word, might also be translated as 'meaning'. Then the verse would run: 'Fundamental to this universe is meaning. The meaning belongs to God, and indeed meaning and God are the same.' This teaching was already implicit in the Old Testament story of the creation and, as I have said, it is taught in all religious views of the world. So we could say that the first great assertion in St John's prologue is simply a re-publication of natural religion and testifies to the continuity between Christianity and the religious faiths of mankind.

But the second truth, the one we have called particular and historical, introduces something new. The meaning that is fundamental to the universe and is indeed identical with God has become flesh, and manifested its glory in a particular human person living in a particular locality at a particular period. This becoming flesh is what is meant by the term 'incarnation'. Christianity has often been called the religion of the incarnation because of the centrality of this idea in its beliefs. Of course, a moment's thought shows us that incarnation could never be understood in a strictly literal way. Flesh, understood literally, is something material; meaning, a word, an idea, are immaterial. So flesh and meaning belong in different categories. The food we eat can literally become flesh through the chemistry of the body, but there is no way that meaning could jump into a quite different category and become a material entity. But the word 'flesh' is used in this passage in a figurative way. 'Flesh' meant the transitory, the finite, the visible and historical, as opposed to the eternal and unseen. In saying that the Word became flesh, it is being claimed that the meaning which had always been in the world now found concrete expression and presence in a particular finite being within the stream of history. That particular finite being was, of course, a human being, for as the prologue also teaches, it is man alone among the creatures who on this earth is the bearer and perceiver of meaning.

24

The Word, then, found its concrete manifestation in a particular human life. But again this must not be pressed too literally. No human person exists in sheer isolation, but only in and through his relations to other persons, and this is true of Jesus Christ as of all other persons. So when we say that the Word was incarnate in Jesus Christ, we cannot mean that it was somehow enclosed within the skin (or the genes) of the man of Nazareth as an individual, but that he was the centre of this event, the boundaries of which cannot be precisely determined in a human social reality extending through both space and time. It is in this sense that we speak of the church as the 'extension of the incarnation'.

The precise boundaries of the event which we call incarnation cannot be determined. This means in turn that the idea of incarnation is not one that we can define with the precision with which we can define a triangle or even a cat. John Hick has remarked that incarnation is not a theory but a mystery. It is not to be described in exact concepts, but can only be hinted at through images or pictures. The idea of incarnation has its origin in a story – the story of a divine being who manifests himself in history as a human being. Such a story we call a 'myth' – not implying that it is untrue, but that its truth is not to be seen in the literal interpretation of the story. Its truth is perceived when we let the story teach us who God is and who man is. Yet it is not satisfactory to say that the gospel witness to Jesus Christ is a myth, for the story which the evangelists tell is also historical, and typically mythological language describes events that cannot be dated. But we declare that Jesus 'suffered under Pontius Pilate', that is to say, at a particular moment in time. According to C. H. Dodd, 'all lines run back to that precise point, which we might date tentatively to Friday, 7 April AD 36'. He adds: 'Not indeed that the exact calendar date is either certain or important . . . but it *is* of some importance that the church remembers an event which is actual, concrete and in principle dateable like any other historical event.'[3]

What has happened is that an event in history (or rather, a series of such events) centred on Jesus of Nazareth has come to be seen as having a depth and universal significance which the church expressed by setting it in the mythological framework of a story of God's dealings with mankind. It is this deeper significance that we mean by the incarnation. This is the response of faith to Jesus Christ, and clearly no amount of historical information about the details of his life could confirm it.

We could also say about incarnation something similar to what Roman Catholic theologians say nowadays about transubstantiation. They say that the word 'transubstantiation' simply affirms the real presence of Christ in the eucharist, without offering any 'explanation'. When we say that God was incarnate in Jesus Christ, we affirm a presence of God in Christ, yes, we affirm that Christ is from God and even in a sense that he *is* God, but this is a mystery of faith, not an empirical fact. A mystery, of course, is not just a blank. It is a truth so deep that we can never exhaust it, and a truth so different from everyday matters of fact that we can speak of it only in indirect allusive language. We have a duty to understand a mystery as far as possible, yet we must also have the wisdom to recognize that the most important truths will always lie beyond the grasp of our finite minds.

Sometimes the church has gone too far in trying to 'explain' the truths of faith in philosophical concepts. There is today, for instance, a widespread reaction against the famous attempt of the early church at the Council of Chalcedon to spell out the incarnation in terms of two natures, a divine and a human, united without either confusion or separation in a single person, the God-man Jesus Christ. The language certainly is both obsolete and needlessly abstract, but the modern critics go much too far in their depreciation of such attempts to put the faith in incarnation into a more systematic language. Those who used such language were just as much concerned for spiritual truth as we are, and we misunderstand them if we think they were engaging only in a metaphysical exercise.

Whatever elucidatory language we may use, the idea of incarnation remains of central importance to us as enshrining some of the deepest truths of Christian faith – truths that have been continuously held if variously expressed since the early days when the disciples confessed that in Jesus Christ the Word had become flesh and that in him they had beheld the glory as of the only Son from the Father. At least three such truths are expressed in a doctrine of incarnation.

The first of these three truths is that in Jesus Christ or, more generally, in the relations between God and man, the initiative lies with God. It is he who comes to us in his humility, not we who rise to him. Of course, in the original experience of the disciples, they attached themselves to the wholly human person, Jesus of Nazareth. They certainly thought of him as a human being long before anyone believed that he was God incarnate. Even after their experiences of the risen Christ had persuaded them that the crucified one was now the Lord of life, they expressed this by saying that God had exalted the man Jesus to his Lordship. All this is important, and must not be forgotten, for otherwise it is easy to forget that Jesus was truly man and we come to think of him as an entirely supernatural being. But as the disciples thought further on the significance of Jesus Christ – and as we too think more deeply on what it would mean for a man to manifest the nature of God – then it becomes clear that a human being could only be exalted to the side of God if God had already taken the initiative and descended into that human being. In this sense we hear the words of St John's gospel: 'No one has ascended into heaven but he who descended from heaven, the Son of Man' (John 3.13). The idea of a man being raised up to God – of being 'adopted' into God, to use a traditional expression – is not opposed to the idea of God's descending into man, the idea of incarnation, but positively demands it.

The second great truth in the idea of incarnation is that of God's deep involvement in and with his creation. If God were simply an exalted being who had created the universe as an arbitrary exercise of power but cared little what would become of it, then of course any thought of incarnation would seem absurd. Unfortunately people often seem to think of God as such an aloof exalted being, and so they do find the belief in incarnation unacceptable. But if we begin from the thought that God created out of love, that the creation is the object of his never-ceasing care and concern, that creation is a sharing and limiting rather than an act of power, then incarnation is so far from being incredible that it could be regarded as the working out of the commitment that God had already made in the beginning. If he cares so deeply, and is so deeply involved with the creation, then what could be more fitting or more germane to his purpose than that he himself should enter the creation in the humble form of a servant, placing himself at the disposal of his creatures so that they might experience in the concrete reality of their own history – in the flesh, to use John's terminology – that God is love rather than power.

The third truth is that this initiative and this involvement have their centre in Jesus Christ. Of course, there is continuity between Christ and the creation, for the same Word is present in each. Yet in Jesus Christ the Word is present with a new concreteness and depth. Why in Jesus Christ rather than elsewhere? There is no answer to this question. It is just one of the givens of history, part of that stream in which we stand, that it is above all in Christ that the presence and reality of God have impinged upon us, so that we confess that in him we have seen the glory as of the only Son from the Father.

Jesus Christ: True Man

Jesus Christ is true man and true God. So we sum up the paradox of the incarnation. In one person, a true humanity and a true divinity have come together in perfect union.

But dare we introduce this word, 'true'? There are many people ready to acknowledge that Christianity is inspiring, challenging, comforting, therapeutic and so on – but could it be in any sense true? Or again, there are many people willing to acknowledge the moral and spiritual stature of Jesus Christ – but can he be truly the God-man, the Word made flesh, the incarnate Lord, or however it may be expressed? It is not hard to persuade many people that there is much in Christianity of the highest worth, but finally we come to the nagging question: Is it true? Many regretfully decide that they cannot believe. That whole complex of belief in God, in the providential action of God in history, in incarnation, in atonement, in resurrection, in a final consummation – all seems so improbable and so remote from the empirical matter-of-fact outlook of our time, that many people turn away. They cannot accept that it is true.

Of course, we cannot ask whether Christianity is true or whether Jesus Christ is true man and true God without facing the deeper question of what truth itself is. How do we know when something is true? When we reflect on this question, we soon perceive that there is no simple answer to it. I believe it to be true that at this moment it is raining heavily in Oxford. I believe it to be true that seven sevens make forty-nine. I believe it to be true that Napoleon was defeated at Waterloo. I believe the theory of evolution to be true. There seem to be many kinds of truth and many ways of testing for truth. Again, some truths can be very easily tested, such as 'It is raining.' Others, like the truth of a complex scientific theory, are much harder to establish.

Some of the truth claims of Christianity are of the same kind as the claims made in purely secular subjects. For instance, the Christian holds some beliefs about Jesus Christ as an historical person – that he lived and died at a particular period of history, that he gave such and such teaching, that he made such and such an impression, that he gave birth to a community and so on. These beliefs about Jesus Christ are of the same kind as the belief that Napoleon was defeated at Waterloo, and New Testament scholars submit them to the same kind of testing as any historian would. But obviously if historical investigation were to demonstrate beyond reasonable doubt that Jesus had lived and taught and died much as the gospels attest, this would hardly touch at all upon the main truth claims that the Christian makes for Christ – that he is the incarnate Word, that he is the Redeemer of mankind, that he is the Resurrection and the life, that he is true man and true God. On the other hand, if investigation were to show beyond reasonable doubt that Jesus Christ never lived at all but was the product of the mythic imagination of some first-century religious sect, what would this say about the truth of Christianity? Some people might say – and some indeed have said – that the Christian truth claim would remain unaffected, for the gospel story is to be understood not as a history but as a parable or myth that teaches the eternal truth of the unity of God and man. But most Christians would be deeply upset, for it might seem to them that when it is deprived of its historical basis, the Christian story loses concreteness and actuality, and that it cannot have these qualities if it is only an inspired fiction. But clearly too they do not equate the truth of the gospel with historical truth.

If we are to get at the meaning of the truth of Christianity, we cannot take isolated parts of it, such as its historical assertions or even its particular doctrines. We have to try to see it and evaluate it as a whole. The Christian faith is not a collection of beliefs, each of which can be judged in isolation. Its beliefs are all interlocking and mutually dependent within a belief system which is co-extensive with life and offers an interpretation of life. It is a vision of life that is rooted in life itself, and above all in the life of Jesus Christ. In him is the central truth that gets spelled out in many derivative truths. St John's gospel reports his claim: 'I am the truth' (John 14.6). This claim indicates that there is a truth more fundamental than the truth of specific historical reports or the truth of doctrinal propositions. This fundamental truth is the truth of a person. This is the ultimate datum of Christian faith, and Christian doctrines are true to the extent that they make accessible to us the living truth of Christ himself.

But what can we possibly mean by the truth of a person or by the claim that Christ is the living truth? I think there is a twofold claim here, corresponding to two aspects that belong to any truth.

The first is the more practical aspect of truth. For truth is that which can be trusted or that which is reliable. This way of thinking of truth is probably the one that was uppermost in the minds of the biblical writers, for in the Semitic languages which they spoke the word for true means literally 'firm' or 'dependable'. The truth is that upon which you can confidently lean. In this sense, Christ is the truth because he is the reliable guide to life, the guide who can be trusted. This is not the kind of truth that can be written down in a book or enunciated in twenty propositions, nor is it the kind of truth that can be instantly appropriated. It is appropriated only through the experience of trying to live in accordance with it. That is why Christ claimed not only to be the truth, but also to be the way and the life. The truth is here inseparable from the way and the life. It is not a truth that can be known from the outside or read off by inspection. It manifests itself as the truth to the extent that it proves itself a reliable guide to the way and the life for human beings, helping them to become more truly persons in a community of persons and to find a meaningful existence.

But truth has a second aspect – the intellectual one. Truth has to do with understanding. If the Semites were for the most part practical in their way of taking truth, the Greeks prized the intellectual aspect. This is apparent even in the word they used for truth, *aletheia*. It is a negative word, meaning literally that which is unconcealed. Truth is the unhiddenness which comes about when something is brought into the light and we see it for what it really is. So when it is said that Christ is the truth, it may be understood in this sense as the claim that he has made something unhidden and has brought into the light something hitherto concealed.

What is it then that Christ thus brings to light? In the first instance, I think we may simply reply: a true humanity. He makes unhidden what human beings have it in them to become. Of all the creatures on earth, man alone has an openness and freedom in his nature, so that he can, within limits, shape his life and character one way or another. He is in search of a true humanity, a condition in which the highest possibilities of his nature will find their fullest expression. There are some ways that do lead towards a truer humanity and a fuller personal life, there are other ways that diminish us. Does anyone, to give examples, believe that the highest possibilities of the human species are brought to light in a Caesar or a Hitler, a Casanova or even a Miss World? But something in Jesus Christ has laid hold on the allegiance of many so that they have confessed him to be the true man. Their consciences have attested that in him is the goal towards which humanity is striving. What do we see in him? Love, freedom, integrity, creativity, moral sensitivity – all these and more. These are the qualities which, *par excellence*, constitute a true humanity. They make Christ true man, man in the truest sense. He is the truth of humanity and personal being.

We claim also that he is true God. Humanity does not exist in a vacuum, and man has not created himself. We have been brought forth by that astonishingly complex and mysterious reality that we call Nature. So far as we know, man is Nature's most highly developed product, and therefore we may believe that humanity is a better clue to the nature of the universe than all the levels of being that lie below man, from the already complex hydrogen atom to the infinitely more complex living organisms that share this planet with man. Now, if Jesus Christ is the true man, the unveiling of the highest possibilities inherent in humanity, then he is the best clue to the creative reality at the heart of our universe, he is the truth of God. He is the Word or meaning that has been there from the beginning and that in him has come to light and been made unconcealed in a decisive way.

Let me now come back to the problems from which this meditation began – the problems which many people have today over the truth of Christian doctrines, perhaps especially the central doctrine of the incarnation. From thinking about the truth of doctrines, we were led on to consider the more fundamental living truth of Christ himself. That truth comes before all the dogmas, scriptures, creeds, classic theological formulations and so on. These are attempts to put into words the truth of Christ, and of necessity they are imperfect attempts, for no form of words can fully express the living personal truth of Christ. But we cannot do without words and language. To the extent that the records, doctrines, creeds and the like point us to Christ and bring him before us – and some of them do this more adequately, some less so – they share in his truth. Without the words of scripture and doctrine, his truth could not be appropriated or communicated by us. We never fully attain to that truth and in its fullness it always escapes our verbal formulations. But we do claim to have glimpsed the fullness of truth in Jesus Christ, and to the extent that our words can express that truth, we affirm their truth. Thus we confess him true man and at the same time true God in human form.

Jesus Christ: True God

We say not only that Jesus Christ is true man but that he is true God as well. But to use the expression 'true God' implies that there must be false gods around. In the present climate of growing understanding among the world religions, it may seem needlessly polemical to assert that there is a 'true God' and that we know this true God in Christ. But to make this claim is not to deny that the true God may be known elsewhere. It is to deny that all conceptions of God are equally valid. There is bad religion as well as good, false gods as well as the true God. The true God has constantly to be distinguished from counterfeits. Sometimes the false gods are in fact the gods of non-Christian religions. In the Old Testament, the God of Israel is always set over against the god of Canaan, and we read, for instance, of the dramatic clash between Elijah, the prophet of the Lord, and the priests of Baal. In the New Testament, Paul contrasts the God whom Christians have known in the Father and the Son with the many gods and many lords of the the pagan world. But false gods are not confined to paganism. Within Christianity itself it has all too often happened, and it still happens, that we set up ideas of God that are the products of our own wishes and imaginations and are far removed from the God and Father of Jesus Christ. But wherever these false ideas of God have come from, they distort the lives and minds of those who worship them.

It was Martin Luther who wrote: 'A god is that to which we look for all good and in which we find refuge in every time of need. To have a god is nothing else than to trust and believe him with our whole heart. The trust and faith of the heart alone make both God and an idol. If your faith and trust are right, then your God is the true God. On the other hand, if your trust is false and wrong, then you have not the true God. For these two belong together, faith and God. That to which your heart clings and entrusts itself is, I say, really your God.'[4]

This is a most important analysis of the meaning, or at least part of the meaning, of the word 'God'. It helps to explain why belief in God or the gods has been so influential in human life. Such a belief is no mere metaphysical theory, but has to do with the things we hold most precious and to which we devote our striving. The influence of such beliefs has often been good and has raised the whole level of human life. But it cannot be denied that often it has been bad and even disastrous, and has degraded life. Many atheists are persons who have been so impressed by the evil consequences of religious belief that they want to get rid of belief in God altogether. No doubt atheism is preferable to false religion, and the modern atheistic critique of faith is something that is needed and that in some ways continues the prophetic denunciations of idolatry in the Old Testament. But atheism remains finally a negative attitude. It may sometimes drive out falsehood, but it remains insensitive to what is true and good in religious faith. And of course the question must be asked, too, whether the atheist does not retain some secret god of his own, in Luther's sense of the word, something which enjoys the trust and faith of his heart and that shapes his life with all the influence of God or an idol.

What is an idol? Paul tells us that idolatry has arisen because men have 'exchanged the truth about God for a lie and worshipped and served the creature rather than the Creator' (Rom. 1.25). The true God who demands from us righteousness and integrity even to the point of suffering and humiliation is too uncomfortable for us. So we put in his place idols that are not God but products of our own wishful thinking, mirroring our creaturely desires and selfish ambitions. What a distance separates the God of the Old Testament with his cry for justice and an end to oppression from the cruel, lustful god of the high places, the *baalim*! And in the New Testament, the contrast is even more starkly drawn between the God-man, Jesus Christ, dying on the cross, and the great pagan gods of the Roman state! As Moltmann truly remarks, the history of Jesus, as theological history, is dominated by the conflict between God and the gods.[5] Here we come to the very heart of the matter. It is a question of love versus power, and that fundamental opposition underlies every conflict between true religion and false, God and the idols. To what does our heart finally cling? What is truly our god? Security and power, or love with all its vulnerability?

According to Justin the Martyr, Jesus was born in a cave near Bethlehem. Since Justin himself was a native of Palestine and writing about a hundred and fifty years after the event, his report might be true. If so, the legend of the child Jesus being born in a stable may not be completely fanciful. In any case, whatever the literal truth may be, the stories are theologically true and touch very closely on the understanding of Jesus Christ as true God. That God should come into history, that he should come in humility, helplessness and poverty – this contradicted everything – this contradicted everything that people had believed about the gods. It was the end of the power deities, the Marduks, the Jupiters, the Akon-Ras, yes, and even of Yahweh, to the extent that he had been misconstrued on the same model. The life that began in a cave ended on the cross, and there was the final conflict between power and love, the idols and the true God, false religion and true religion. Yet we have to confess that it was not the final conflict. The God of Jesus Christ, like Yahweh before him, has been turned back again and again into a God of war or the God of the nation or the patron of a culture. The tendency to idolatry is apparently as strong among Christians as among pagans.

The early Christians did not believe that an idol is just an inanimate object, a sculptured piece of stone or metal. They believed that every idol is the seat of a demon. To quote Justin on this topic, he says 'we not only deny that the idols are gods, but assert that they are wicked and impious demons'. There is, of course, a true insight in this, a much deeper insight than that of the shallow modern rationalist who supposes that you can dispose of false gods (and perhaps true ones as well!) by saying that they don't exist. They *do exist*; most certainly so, if we remember Luther's words that your God is 'that to which your heart clings and entrusts itself'. An idol or false god is not just nothing. It has the dark menacing superhuman power of a demon.

Let me not be misunderstood when I say this. I was one of the Anglican theologians who urged the bishops of the Church of England not to give any official recognition to the practice of exorcism in the church. I have been much distressed by the recrudescence in recent years of belief in demon possession and of an unhealthy interest in the occult. In saying that the fathers had a true insight when they claimed that false gods are demons, I did not mean that there are alien evil spirits abroad in the world. One of the great blessings of science is that it has freed us from the dark paralysing fear that demons are lurking all around intent on doing us harm. It is hard for us to imagine the oppressive terror which afflicted people of a former age – and still afflicts people in some parts of the world

today – because it is believed that the whole environment is populated with unseen malevolent powers. In *The Golden Bough* Sir James Frazer wrote of deliverance from the demons in these words: 'For ages the army of spirits, once so near, has been receding further and further from us, banished by the magic wand of science from hearth and home, from ruined cell and ivied tower, from haunted glade and lonely mere ... Only in poets' dreams or impassioned flights of oratory is it given to catch a glimpse of the last flutter of the standards of the retreating host, to hear the beat of their invisible wings, the sound of their mocking laughter.'[6] Perhaps nowadays we would have to say 'in bishops' dreams' rather than 'in poets' dreams', but in any case, it has been a merciful deliverance, and I do not think we would wish it otherwise.

But few people would be so foolish as to claim that because a particular way of explaining some of the dark superhuman evils of the world had been abandoned, these evils themselves had been overcome or had grown less or had even been fully understood. There are today in human affairs evils so gigantic and threats so intractable that they can rightly be called demonic. They seem to have acquired a momentum of their own and to have withdrawn themselves from human control. But we need not lay them at the door of supposed alien spirits, any more than we might blame the influence of the stars. Although they are now apparently beyond human control, it is we ourselves who have spawned them and given them their power. They are the fruits of idolatry, of worshipping and serving the creature rather than the Creator, of letting our hearts cling to that which is less than God and even opposed to God. It is in this sense that the early Christians were right in linking the idols and the demons.

Exorcism is of no use here. Indeed, exorcism is like atheism, a negative phenomenon that seeks to attack the evil but does not get to the heart of the problem, which is to replace evil by good. And this means we have got to be able to discriminate between the two, and know where the good lies. We find it in Jesus Christ. He is true God, for the love we see in him is the truth of God, and stands in judgment over against all the idolatrous cults of power and indulgence. All our thinking about God must be conformed to the Christ who was born in a cave and died on a cross.

The early Christians believed that they could drive out demons by making the sign of the cross. Alas, with us this has too often become a shallow gesture. But if it does mean a true affirmation of the cross, a confession that the true nature of God is present in the love and humility of Christ and not in all the impressive powers arrayed against him, if it means that our hearts really cling to him and take him as our true God, then this is the real exorcism and the way to healing and new life in the human family. It is the breaking of the power of the idols and the freedom of serving the true God.

3

THE TEACHING

The evangelists have preserved for us much of the teaching of Jesus, and even people who are unwilling or unable to join with Christians in confessing the Lordship of Jesus Christ are often ready to acknowledge the depth and power of his teaching. Some people in his own time called him a rabbi, others a prophet, but this teacher fits into no readymade category. He taught with an authority and convincingness that made him stand out from other teachers. Above all, his teaching was at one with his living and dying.

That teaching of Jesus covered many topics but here we are going to reflect on only a few – those that have to do with his understanding of God and especially of what we have called the humility of God.

Providence

The writers of the Bible clearly believed that God acts in the world. Indeed, the Bible has been called the recital of the acts of God, and a God who did not act would be a somewhat redundant deity. But how does he act? There was not always agreement on this question, and it is still discussed.

There is an incident in the gospels that shows us what the popular understanding of God's action was, and how Jesus sought to correct it. 'There were present at that very time some who told him of the Galileans whose blood Pilate had mingled with their sacrifices. And he answered them, "Do you think that these Galileans were worse sinners than all the other Galileans, because they suffered thus? . . . Or those eighteen on whom the tower in Siloam fell, do you think that they were worse offenders than all the others who dwelt in Jerusalem? I tell you, No; but unless you repent, you will all likewise perish"' (Luke 13.1-5). It would be easy to bring this passage up to date, by substituting for the Galileans the Ugandan Christians whose blood General Amin has mingled with their eucharists; or for the eighteen on whom the tower fell, the thousands that have been buried beneath collapsing buildings in earthquakes in China, Romania and elsewhere; and we could add new categories, such as the thousands more who have perished in recent times in air and road accidents. Such occasions of dramatic suffering have always been part of the texture of human history. And people have always asked why such events happen.

Perhaps it is senseless to ask why. These things just happen – there will always be cruel tyrants ready to slaughter the innocent, there will always be natural hazards of earthquake and storm and flood, together with new hazards arising out of man's technology. This is just the way things are in an imperfect world. But the person who believes in God will not be able to dismiss the question why such things happen as senseless. To believe in God is to believe that there is some sense and meaning in history and some providential governance of the universe. Thus whatever seems to contradict such a belief constitutes a problem. It puts a question mark opposite our belief in a God who is supposed to be wise and just and loving and powerful. Perhaps, however, it is already an indication of our prejudices and misunderstandings about God that we tend to look for an 'act of God' chiefly in some unforeseen disaster.

For many centuries there were people who believed that they did know the answer to the question why some human beings suffer in a signal manner. They suffered, so it was believed, because they were being punished by God. Some terrible sin had been committed, perhaps not even by the victims of the catastrophe themselves, but by their forefathers, but now fate had caught up with them. I use the word 'fate' deliberately, because this really was a fatalistic view and conceived God's justice as nothing more than an inflexible and impersonal principle of retribution.

But apart from anything else, that way of understanding God's action simply does not square with the observed facts. It is not usually the wicked or the descendants of the wicked who are the obvious sufferers. It is oftener the other way round. The Galileans who suffered under Pilate and the Christians who have suffered under modern regimes were people of simple human dignity and piety who were sacrificed to tyrannical cruelty or ideological fanaticism. The Romanians and Chinese who perished in the earthquakes were presumably no worse than Britons and West Germans.

Long before the time of Christ, thinking men in Israel were already turning away from the idea that disasters come upon the people through the operation of an inflexible destiny. The Book of Job challenged the correlation of suffering and sin. Various prophets developed the idea of individual responsibility before God. So Jesus was not teaching anything new when he declined to agree with the popular belief that the sufferers in his own time had been selected by God for an exemplary exercise of the divine power. Jesus certainly believed in the providential activity of God, but he taught people to see it not in the dramatic and terrifying but in such ordinary events as the growth of the flowers and the life of the birds and so by implication in the daily life of man himself.

But we are driven back to the question: How does God act in the world? What part does he play in history? How does he lead and sustain men in their lives? Jews and Christians alike believe that God does act in the world and that he shapes the ends of history. As I said already, a God who does nothing and is impotent in his own creation would hardly deserve to count as God at all. But once the idea has been given up that God's action is to be seen in dramatic events and that he keeps intervening in the course of history, judging, punishing, rewarding, we have to look for his action in more subtle and ambiguous manifestations. And it will hardly do either to say that God is acting in everything that occurs, for although this might be true in the sense that he is the source and originator of everything, the idea of his acting would become a vacuous notion if it could be applied indifferently to everything that happens. So we have to face the question of how we can conceive his action in the world, and if we cannot give some reasonably clear answer to the question, then can we go on talking about a God of history, of a sense and meaning and goal in history, or of a moral government of the universe?

I think the question is even more difficult for us today than it was when men were disputing the nature of God's actions in biblical times, for nowadays most historians – even church historians – write history as if God has no part in it at all. Like the physicist Laplace, it seems that the modern historian has no need of the God hypothesis.

39

Historians account for the course of events in terms of human decisions, on the one hand, and social, economic, psychological, even climatic factors, on the other hand. Events within the historical process are explained in terms of other events that are immanent in the same process. There seems to be no place at all for any divine action in this closely knit texture. Indeed, sometimes human decisions are themselves played down and there emerges a new fatalism or determinism, though now it is no longer God but, let us say, economics that becomes the all-powerful controller of world events. Sometimes it is argued too that even our beliefs are strictly determined by sociological and cultural influences, though this would seem to lead into a self-destroying scepticism.

Yet in the face of all this, I would say, God does act. I do not mean just that he acted in the beginning by starting up the process of the creation, as the deists of the Enlightenment believed, nor do I mean that his action is simply a diffuse energy through all events. God acts, and acts quite specifically, in human history and in the life-stories of individuals. To be sure, he does not act by causing earthquakes to punish the wicked or by stirring up tyrants to persecute his people as a judgment on their backslidings. He acts on a far deeper and more personal level, by appeal, by attraction, by drawing people out of themselves and towards himself.

The old idea that God was a kind of *deus ex machina* who intervened sporadically in human affairs when something needed putting right, or again that he exercised an immediate moral government of the universe, came to be abandoned, as we have noted, when some of the Hebrew prophets began to understand the meaning of responsibility and so broke away from such ideas as inherited guilt and automatic retribution. It is in a world of free, responsible, to some extent autonomous beings, that the idea of God's action has to be conceived and takes on a new significance. God's action does not infringe the responsibility or freedom of man. Rather, it is the grace that draws man precisely into a fuller freedom and dignity. Hence the familiar words of the Prayer Book, that God's service is 'perfect freedom'.

The great act of God on this earthly scene was, we Christians believe, his presence in Jesus Christ, the incarnate Word. In Christ he came not as Supreme Disposer, but as the one of whom human beings disposed; not as the avenger of past sins, but as the pioneer of a new future for mankind; not as compulsive power, but as what men take for weakness, though it is more truly called creative love. This was the climax of God's acting, and it is in the light of this great act that we recognize all the other acts of his, even something so apparently commonplace as the clothing of the lilies.

Still today wherever Christ is held up, whether in the Word or the sacraments or simply in the loving and liberating deed, we know God's action in our lives and we feel him drawing us too into the same renewing way of love. This truly personal action of God upon us is surely far more impressive than what was visualized in those old fatalistic beliefs that some preordained retribution, some principle of *karma*, had already determined the course of our lives and the shape of our society and what destiny is possible for us. It is true that we still feel the burden of the past and have all known the sense of helplessness in the face of forces that seem to have got beyond human control. We have all felt at one time or another stifled and frustrated. Yet we have known too the moments of freedom and the visions of deliverance. It is at such times that we must remember God himself coming apparently helpless in Jesus Christ into the clash of the principalities and powers – apparently helpless, I say, but strong in faith and hope and love to break down the imprisoning walls and to create a new situation of openness. There is nothing magical about this, yet it is nothing less than a new creation. It is at such moments that we catch a glimpse in our lives of the inexhaustible depth and mystery of the divine action. This is how God acts among us, not by compulsion but by an appeal that respects the gifts of freedom and responsibility which he has himself given us in the sharing act of creation. It remains for us to turn and lay hold on the new opportunities which he offers.

Prayer

The disciples came to Jesus and requested, 'Lord, teach us to pray.' He responded by teaching them what we call the Lord's Prayer: 'Our Father, who art in heaven, hallowed be thy name. Thy kingdom come. Thy will be done, on earth as it is in heaven. Give us this day our daily bread. And forgive us our trespasses, as we forgive those that trespass against us. And lead us not into temptation, but deliver us from evil. For thine is the kingdom, the power and the glory for ever. Amen.' In St Luke's gospel, there is associated with the prayer a saying of the Lord: 'Ask, and it will be given you; seek, and you will find; knock, and it will be opened to you. For everyone who asks receives, and he who seeks finds, and to him who knocks it will be opened' (Luke 11.9–10).

Many people nowadays have problems with prayer, and especially they have problems with prayer understood as asking. Perhaps they feel that there is something childish in asking anything of God. Has not the human race outgrown its dependence on God? We should do things for ourselves, and be ashamed to fall back to God. Thus Nietzsche's Zarathustra exclaims: 'Prayer is shameful! The cowardly devil within thee that would . . . have things made easier – this devil persuadeth thee, "There *is* a God!" ' [7] Yet the instinct to pray to God seems to be so deeply rooted in man that even very sophisticated persons find themselves praying in sudden emergencies. Of course, this may happen only through a regrettable lapse or loss of nerve, and no one would wish to defend prayer as simply the last resource to which people unthinkingly turn when everything else has failed.

On the other hand, among many people there has been a considerable revival of interest in prayer in recent years. But it must be noted that this contemporary interest in prayer is rather different from what has been usually understood as prayer in earlier times. People today are attracted to prayers of meditation and contemplation, but not to prayers of asking. They find it easier to understand and justify meditation and contemplation. Such prayers concentrate the mind, strengthen the will, heighten sensitivity, enrich experience and so on. Such points are generally agreed. There are many people who might call themselves agnostics or humanists who nevertheless engage in some kind of meditation, and even if they do not call this prayer, it is very close to forms of prayer that have been used in Christian spirituality. Iris Murdoch, for instance, has written eloquently of the value of 'attending to the good' in the moral life. [8] There is, she maintains, a place both inside and outside religion for letting the mind dwell on that which has highest claim upon us. It does seem clear that fixing our attention on the good helps to orient the whole person towards it and strengthens the will in the pursuit of it.

One should notice, however, that these modern attitudes imply quite a reversal. Traditionally, the prayer of asking was the first rung in the ladder of prayer. Meditation and, even more, contemplation, were further up the ladder. These were higher levels of prayer, to which one might eventually attain, but most people would be likely to remain on the supposedly lower levels. But now meditation seems to come at the beginning. It is not regarded as an 'advanced' form of prayer, but the kind that seems most natural to a modern sophisticated person.

Clearly, meditation and contemplation do have a value that appeals both to believers and non-believers, and they are practices in which people can honestly engage without very much in the way of explicit religious belief. They are to be further valued just because they form a kind of spiritual link between Christians and non-Christians – for instance, one could visualize meditative prayers for peace in which both groups could join. But the modern preference for meditation must not blind us to the fact that Christian prayer has always been basically a prayer of asking. When the disciples asked Jesus to teach them to pray, he did not respond by advising them to meditate on the good nor did he teach them sophisticated techniques of contemplation. He told them to ask, to seek, to knock; and the model prayer that he taught them is one that consists of a series of petitions. It is quite unmistakably a prayer of asking.

In the teaching of Jesus Christ, therefore, the primary meaning of prayer is asking. In the modern situation, we may find that embarrassing, but I do not think we can get away from it. Indeed, prayers of petition, supplication, intercession have from the beginning had a prominent place both in the public liturgy of the church and in the private devotions of individual Christians. We cannot even repeat the Lord's Prayer without affirming, through our very act of repeating it, our commitment to that kind of prayer. Yet the difficulties and questionings that people experience concerning prayer as asking are serious ones. If we cannot solve their problems by telling them to give up asking and to be content with meditation, neither can we solve them by saying that this is how Jesus taught his disciples or that this is something that the church has always done. We have to try to understand the matter on a deeper level.

Let us first of all take note of some of the questions and objections that trouble people when they reflect on the prayer of asking. Is not the prayer of asking the first childish level of prayer, so that eventually we have to put it behind us and graduate to meditative and contemplative levels of prayer? Does not the prayer of asking imply a naive idea of God, as some arbitrary ruler who can be persuaded through prayer to intervene in the events of the world and to order them the way we want them? Is there not a lingering magic endemic in this prayer of asking, an attempt to manipulate God? Does it not encourage sloth, by teaching us to rely on God to do things that we ought to be doing for ourselves? How do we know what to ask for? We are, after all, such self-centred creatures and our horizons are so narrow that the prayer of asking is almost bound to be cramped by our own limitations, and such prayer will be confining rather than liberating. In any case, if God already knows better than we do ourselves what is good for us and for the world at large, what is the point in asking him?

Some of these questions do draw our attention to genuine difficulties that have to be faced. It is all too easy for us to ask the wrong things and to let our petitions be narrowly circumscribed by our own desires, interests and prejudices. This can obviously happen on the level of the individual and his prayers, but one sometimes hears public intercessions that have more than a hint of propaganda (theological or political) infused into them. But consideration of these dangers leads us to an important truth about prayer. *The prayer of asking must always be closely related to the prayer of meditation.* This is the only way to ensure that our asking will not be distorted by our personal preferences and prejudices. It is significant that in the public liturgy, the prayers of the faithful come after the ministry of the word. It is after their minds have been exposed to the word that the people are ready to make their petitions. For in meditation, we immerse ourselves in the substance of the Christian faith, and as we come to understand it better and so to understand better the mind and will of Christ himself, then our prayers of asking will be increasingly purged from whatever is unworthy or egotistical or partisan in them.

Likewise, it is all too easy for us to pray, let us say, for peace or for the unfortunate, and to leave it at that. But true prayer can never encourage sloth. It must rather excite the desire to be God's agents for the fulfilling of the prayer. Prayer never delivers us from action directed towards the end of the prayer. Indeed, prayer would be little more than hypocrisy if it did not issue in such action, and the prayer of asking is only justifiable if we are honestly striving ourselves to realize its objective.

The questions just considered do have their point, and should compel us to be more thoughtful and honest in our prayers of asking. But some of the other questions and difficulties I mentioned earlier really rest on a misunderstanding – a misunderstanding both of prayer and of the God to whom that prayer is addressed. I mean, questions like 'Is it not childish to ask anything from God?' and 'Is not prayer a kind of magic?' Such questions betray a misunderstanding of prayer, because those who ask them think of prayer as an attempt to bend or influence the divine will in accordance with human wishes, to coax or persuade God into doing something which he might not otherwise have done. Equally, these questions betray a misunderstanding of God, for they think of him as the arbitrary disposer of events, acting from outside so as to direct events one way or another, whereas he is already in the very stream of events and seeking to realize his good purposes for his creatures. But these purposes are often frustrated and nullified by the sinful wills of human beings, for to them God has given freedom even to defy himself.

Properly understood, then, petitionary prayer has nothing to do with trying to manipulate the divine will or to influence God; on the contrary, it is concerned with bending our own wills to God and letting his Spirit influence us, so that the hindrances that we put in his way are removed and his good purposes given free course among his creatures. Prayer is the establishing of a communion between God and the finite centres of freedom in his creation, so that the creatures will work with God for the fulfilment of his creation. God already knows what is for the good of his creatures and he is already seeking it – he does not wait for us to ask him. Our prayers are not intended to persuade him to seek the good of his creatures, but to help us to align our wills with his so that his good purpose can come to effect.

We can apply this understanding of prayer to the specific kind of asking which we call intercession, that is to say, prayers for others. Sometimes they are others whom we know well, sometimes they are others whom we have never seen and who may live at a great distance from us. We may be praying that they may be healed of sickness or delivered from violence or sustained in adversity or preserved in peace. Is it possible to believe that our prayers can make any difference to their situation?

Most Christians, I believe, would not be satisfied with the explanation that our prayers make us more concerned or more compassionate towards those for whom we pray. It is true that our prayers do that, and this is both valuable and important. But we believe that there is more to it, and I think this belief is justified. In our time, we are learning as never before the solidarity of the whole human race.

None of us are islands. Our lives interpenetrate at many points. We are bound together by innumerable ties, some of them scarcely understood, so that what happens in one part of humanity cannot fail to influence what happens in another part. If even a small number of people are interceding before God, we may say that a way is being provided into that dense texture of human relationships in which we are all bound up. An opening has been made so that the divine will can have access. And since God's will is for peace and health and wholeness, prayer can be a dynamic transforming force among the race of men.

With those thoughts in mind, let us look again at that model prayer which our Lord taught to the disciples, a prayer of asking which can be taken as a norm against which to judge all our petitions to God. The petitions of the Lord's Prayer are entirely free of any self-centredness or any narrowness of interest or any desire to influence God. They look to the coming of his kingdom and the doing of his will, for these contain all possible good for his creatures, more than we could ever imagine or express.

It is good that in recent times the value of meditation has been rediscovered by many, but alongside the meditative type of prayer the more basic prayer of asking, as taught by Christ, still has its place and still makes sense.

Liberation

One of the most popular words among Christians in recent years has been the word 'liberation'. We have heard much of 'liberation theologies' which sometimes concern themselves with the liberation of particular social or ethnic groups, sometimes with liberation in general. Jesus has been cast in the role of liberator, an archetypal Simon Bolivar, so to speak. We have heard such slogans as 'Jesus means freedom' and 'Jesus Christ frees and unites', though it must be said that oversimplified assertions of that sort are more confusing than enlightening. More soberly, Jesus has been called the truly free man who sets others free (Paul van Buren). All this, moreover, is usually given a strongly political slant.

However, when we consider the actual teaching of Jesus, there is hardly any mention of freedom. It is true that, according to Luke, at the outset of his ministry he gave a kind of inaugural sermon in the synagogue at Nazareth on a passage from Isaiah: 'The Spirit of the

Lord is upon me, because he has anointed me to preach good news to the poor. He has sent me to proclaim release to the captives and recovering of sight to the blind, to set at liberty those who are oppressed, to proclaim the acceptable year of the Lord' (Luke 4.16–19). But what Jesus thought about freedom is not to be derived from his teaching but rather from his way of life. He showed freedom towards the law, when this was taken in a legalistic way. He was free in his choice of company, and not bound by social conventions. Yet, as Bonhoeffer noted, there is no reason to suppose that he was at all concerned with political freedom.

In the New Testament, explicit teaching on freedom is found not in the words of Jesus but in the writings of Paul and John. It is Paul who speaks of 'the glorious liberty of the children of God' (Rom. 8.21) and of Christian freedom in the face of law and tradition (Gal. 5). In John's gospel Jesus is represented as saying, 'You will know the truth, and the truth will make you free' (John 8.32), but these words were not intended in the modern sense to mean that truth enlightens and liberates the mind. Specifically, it was the truth of Jesus Christ, and the liberation was to be liberation from the slavery of sin.

Still, when these reservations are made, we can acknowledge that it is a true instinct that connects Jesus Christ with liberation. He sums up in himself and deepens whatever is affirmative in the earlier biblical tradition, and freedom certainly had a central place in that. The God of Israel was a liberating God, for the great formative event in the history of the first people of God, an event which they continued (and still continue) to celebrate all through the succeeding centuries, was their deliverance from the slavery and oppression of Egypt. 'We were Pharaoh's slaves in Egypt; and the Lord brought us out of Egypt with a mighty hand' (Deut. 6.21). The story of that deliverance has been a source of inspiration and hope to many oppressed peoples since, and they have made their own the cry, 'Let my people go!' and have understood God as the liberating power in history.

Still, liberation or setting free, considered in itself, is not an idea that conveys very much to us. This is because it is in the main a negative idea, and needs to be filled in with content. Liberation is the dissolving of a false relation, but it remains incomplete until a new relation comes into being and takes the place of the old one. This negativity goes back to freedom itself. Although freedom is something that we prize very highly, it is in a sense nothing at all – it is

47

precisely the free area, the empty room, not yet filled up and determined but available to us. Thus talk of freedom or of liberation always needs to be specified. What is one made free *from*? More importantly still, what is one made free *for*? There are many liberation movements at the present time, but one often has the feeling that a word is being bandied about without much understanding, and in fact there can be no true liberation without an understanding both of freedom from and freedom for. Presumably liberation theology has the task of specifying these matters with reference to Jesus Christ. He it is who gives depth and definite content to the abstract idea of liberation.

Let us begin with freedom from . . . From what is Jesus himself, the truly free man, free? He is not free from the things of which many people want to be free. He is not free from suffering. He is not free from the social and political forces which surround him and eventually send him to his death. He is not free from poverty and hardship – he does not even have a place to lay his head. And so we could go on. From what then is he free? The New Testament answers the question plainly enough by telling us he was free from sin. This is the fundamental freedom from . . . For it is sin that distorts and enslaves human existence and separates it from its creative source in God. Sinful man is turned in on himself in self-concern. He is imprisoned in himself. Jesus is the free man who sets others free because he is not concerned or anxious for himself or his interests.

What is Jesus free *for*, and what does he let us be free *for*? Again, I think the answer is fairly plain, and follows from what we have already been saying. Jesus is free for the other, and he lets us be free for the other. He is the available man. The gospels give the impression that he was also a busy man, with many pressing in upon him, but we all know from experience that it is usually the busy man who can make himself free and available when we need him. He is likely to be busy because he is not always glancing anxiously at the clock, wondering if he has time for this or that.

We can add here also that Jesus was free for death. People have always wanted to be free *from* death, but how rarely are people free *for* death! Christ's prayer in the garden, 'Not my will but yours!' is not only a great prayer. It is a great act of freedom, though paradoxically it is at the same time an act of submission. Jesus' freedom for death is a special case of his freedom for the other – to be precise, his availability to God.

48

The freedom of Jesus, then, is very different from what we commonly understand as freedom. Indeed, he reverses our usual notions on the subject. He gives to the empty ideas of freedom and liberation a content which surprises us, yet which we perceive to be freedom and liberation at their deepest. And is this not because in Jesus we see the freedom of God himself? When we talk of God's sovereign freedom, we usually think this means that he can do whatever he pleases in his omnipotence, just as we think our own freedom might consist in the power to fulfil all our desires. But God's freedom is his freedom for us – his coming out from himself and his availability.

Reconciliation

Reconciliation has a fundamental place in the teaching of Jesus. To be sure, the actual word is not much used by him or by other New Testament writers, but the reality is at the very heart of Christianity. Reconciliation means a deep change in the relations between two people or groups of people, a change in which enmity and alienation are replaced by peace and mutual acceptance. How important reconciliation is in Jesus' teaching can be seen from his words: 'If you are offering your gift at the altar, and there remember that your brother has something against you, leave your gift there before the altar and go; first be reconciled to your brother, and then come and offer your gift' (Matt. 5.23–24).

In this matter as in others, Jesus' teaching is closely connected with his own career, and in Paul's writings it is Christ himself, and especially his cross, that effect reconciliation. This reconciliation takes place on two levels. There is reconciliation between God and man, and there is the reconciliation of human beings among themselves. These two dimensions of reconciliation cannot be separated. According to Paul, 'in Christ, God was reconciling the world to himself'; Paul describes his own ministry as a 'ministry of reconciliation', and the essence of his preaching is: 'We beseech you on behalf of Christ, be reconciled to God' (II Cor. 5.18–20). The other side of this reconciliation is seen in the new community about which we learn in Ephesians, the coming together through Christ in one body and one humanity of the thitherto alienated groups of Jews and Gentiles. 'For he is our peace, who has made us both one, and has broken down the dividing wall of hostility . . . that he might reconcile us both to God in one body through the cross, thereby bringing the hostility to an end' (Eph. 2.14–16). Athanasius probably had this passage in mind when more than two hundred years later he wrote: 'Only on the cross does one die with hands outstretched; therefore the Lord had to endure this and stretch out his hands, that with the one he might draw the ancient people and with the other those of the Gentiles, and that he might join both in himself.'[9]

There is no doubt that reconciliation is central to Christianity, and there is no doubt either that in the world today, with all its deep divisions, reconciliation is sorely needed. Yet it seems to be the case that at the present time the idea of reconciliation is regarded with some suspicion, even among Christians. Some time ago I attended a gathering of Anglican churchmen from all over the world, meeting in Trinidad, and one of the local clergy said to me, '"Reconciliation" is not a good word in the Caribbean.' This remark reflects the tone of a good many books that have been written in recent years on the subject of political theology, as it is called. With a few important exceptions (to one of which I shall refer later) these books have very little to say about reconciliation. On the other hand, their vocabulary is typically laden with words like 'liberation', 'polarization', 'struggle', 'protest' and the like. The same mood is reflected in other religious writings. A recent book on the Blessed Virgin Mary by a feminist of Roman Catholic background deplores her influence on the place of women in society because she presents an image of submissiveness and domesticity, and apparently considers that she would have done much better if she had been as abrasive and self-assertive as the author herself appears to be. Even in some ecumenical circles, the word 'reconciliation' has gone out of favour. One no longer speaks of the reconciliation of churches or ministries, but of their recognition, a word which suggests the assertion of a right.

Of course, for a long time critics of Christianity have argued that its stress on love, humility, meekness, non-aggression, has been harmful to mankind. Marx claimed that Christianity lulls the people into a condition of contentment with their lot and prevents them from struggling for its betterment. A major difference between Christians and Marxists is that the Marxists have no use for reconciliation but aim at what they call the 'liquidation' of their opponents. Likewise to Nietzsche the Christian preoccupation with love and peace seemed to be a sign of weakness and decadence. The only true peace, he maintained, is victory. In such avowed enemies of Christianity as Marx and Nietzsche, it is not surprising to find such criticisms. But it is surprising to find them echoed in Christian writers, and suggests that there has been something wrong or inadequate in the church's teaching about reconciliation.

One can surely acknowledge right away that often reconciliation has been understood in too superficial a way. It is significant that Paul links reconciliation so firmly to the cross, for true reconciliation is achieved only at the highest price. I said that reconciliation means a profound change in the relations between the persons concerned, and where that change is less than profound, there has been no true reconciliation. The reconciliation that is suspect and the target for criticism is only a counterfeit reconciliation. The deep relation has not been changed, there have been only some superficial adjustments and perhaps worse trouble is being stored up for the future. A merely sentimental Christianity deserves all the criticisms that have been made against it.

A true reconciliation is not based on sentiment or weakness or spinelessness. Neither is it incompatible with anger. Perhaps Christians ought to feel anger oftener than they do, in the face of tyranny, injustice, hypocrisy and many other evils. Paul and even our Lord could use pretty abusive language on occasion. I do not myself feel uncomfortable when reciting or singing those psalms which express indignation against genocide, sacrilege and the like. On the other hand, I do feel uncomfortable when, for instance, as often happens nowadays, I am expected to go directly from Psalm 82 to Psalm 84, that is to say, to 'How lovely is thy dwelling place!' missing out Psalm 83 which is a strongly worded denunciation of genocide. Unhappily, genocide is as much a reality in the world as lovely dwelling places, and if we do not get angry about that, then surely our Christianity is getting soft and sentimental.

The biblical writers even speak of the anger of God against whatever outrages his righteousness, but God is not content to be angry or to destroy – he moves towards costly reconciliation. For Christians too, indignation, struggle, conflict are sometimes right, but they can be only stages on the way to the ultimate goal of reconciliation. Still, they may be necessary stages if that reconciliation is not to be superficial, but a really deep coming together.

There is another problem about trying to apply the Christian remedy of reconciliation in the world today. In the New Testament, reconciliation is understood in relation to individuals or small groups, that is to say, in personal and interpersonal terms. We can understand reconciliation among a small group of Christians of different ethnic or racial background, or reconciliation with the friend or colleague whom we have offended. But how does one bring about reconciliation between, let us say, blacks and whites in southern Africa, or Catholics and Protestants in Ulster, or in any other case where large numbers of people are involved and their relations have become very impersonal? Here we are likely to be told that reconciliation is unrealistic, that the problem is political and can be solved only by coercion. We hear a good deal nowadays about the political duty of the Christian, but politics is very much an area of conflict where 'coalition' is a bad word and polarization seems to be increasing in most countries. Abraham Heschel complained that 'the pestilence of our day is the dehumanization of politics'.

To one South American 'liberation' theologian, it is all fairly simple. He divides the human race into 'good guys' and 'bad guys', the oppressed and the oppressors, and claims that it is the inescapable duty of the Christian to join the political struggle on the side of the good guys. Most Christians, however, will think that the scene is a good deal more complicated than that. The conflicts that he sees going on around him are very ambiguous, and often it is not clear that he has any Christian duty to take one side or the other. Jacques Ellul, noting that in many of the conflicts of our time sincere Christians are to be found on both sides, welcomes this fact, for he claims that their Christianity can unite them across political and partisan divisions, so lessening the hostility of those divisions and preparing the way for eventual reconciliation.

One further point that we must not forget is that the New Testament understanding of reconciliation has two dimensions – the relation to God as well as the relation among human beings. It is that relation to God that relativizes every human situation and every human cause, and prevents us from making the claim that in any human conflict, the good is to be found entirely on one side and the evil on the other. Sin is present in all human life, though not always to the same degree. Perhaps then human relations can only come right when we have all come into a right relation to God. The same South American theologian whom I criticized a moment ago says in another part of his book that 'liberation from sin is at the very root of political liberation', and with this we can heartily agree.

But I want to leave the last word to another liberation theologian who has been in a remarkable way sensitive both to the complexities of our modern problems and to the difficult vocation of the Christian in the midst of them. I mean James Deotis Roberts, an exponent of the black theology of the United States. Two sentences of his will summarize most of what needs to be said, and they are taken from a book with the significant title, *Liberation and Reconciliation*. One sentence is: 'There can be no shortcut to reconciliation that does not pass through liberation.' With that he dismisses all the sentimental easy-going Christianity that only pretends to reconcile but does not face the deep and costly changes that belong to true reconciliation through the cross. But the second sentence is: '[Liberation] however rewarding to set the record straight, cannot be an ultimate Christian goal and must give way to reconciliation.'[10] With that he rebukes those who glorify struggle and conflict and points us to the true goal. It is a difficult goal and the way to it is the painful way of the cross, but it is supremely worthwhile.

4

THE PASSION

After a ministry of teaching and healing in the countryside, Jesus set his face towards Jerusalem, the seat of the religious and political establishment. What did he hope to accomplish there? We cannot know what may have been in his mind, but we do know that his journey ended on the cross. But Christians believe that this was not just the death of a good man who deserved a better fate; they have seen in these events of the passion God's own costly involvement in his creation and the opening of a way to a new life for the human race.

The Passion in Prospect

How did Jesus himself understand his last journey to Jerusalem and the events that befell him there? How did he face his suffering and death, and what meaning did he see in these events?

The traditional answer to these questions is well known. After having been acknowledged as the Messiah by his disciples, Jesus 'began to teach them that the Son of man must suffer many things and be rejected by the elders and the chief priests and the scribes, and be killed, and after three days rise again' (Mark 8.31). These words from the gospel record seem to imply that Jesus was fully aware of his messianic vocation, that he knew that this vocation must be fulfilled through suffering and death, and also that after three days he would rise from the dead. This is how the gospels themselves present the story, and throughout most of its history the church has believed both that Christ had foreknowledge of his passion and death and that he understood them as a necessary part of the mission that he had to fulfil. Some theologians have gone so far as to claim that even in the womb of the Virgin, from the very moment of his conception, he had a perfect understanding of these matters. Others have been modest in their claims, and have argued that he must have grown up gradually into the understanding of his mission, but most of them too have believed that he went to his death as something that he had clearly foreseen and which he understood as essential to the work of the Messiah. He saw himself as the suffering servant described by the prophet, 'despised and rejected by men, a man of sorrows and acquainted with grief . . . wounded for our transgressions . . . bruised for our iniquities' (Isa. 53.3, 5).

Yet once we begin to think about it, we see that this traditional way of understanding Jesus' intention in going to Jerusalem and his attitude to the suffering and death that came upon him there is one that raises many serious problems.

The most serious of all these problems concerns the true humanity of Christ. If Jesus Christ has any relevance to the human condition and is the true mediator between man and God, then he must have fully shared our human condition, that is to say, he must have been fully man. But it is most certainly a part of the human condition that we do *not* foresee the future – at least, not in any detailed way. Thus, if Jesus indeed foresaw his passion and death and – still more – his resurrection, would this not amount to a denial of his true humanity? Would it not turn him into a wholly supernatural figure who only appeared to be human? From very early times, the church has been tempted to the so-called 'docetic' heresy, the belief that Jesus only 'looked like' a man but was really a wholly divine being with only the external appearance of being human. Sometimes men may have thought of Christ in that way with the intention of doing him greater honour. I suspect that more often a subconscious motive has been at work – men have thought of Christ in this docetic way because it removes him to a safe distance. We shall not find him nearly so disturbing or challenging if we have decided that he is not really one of ourselves but a being from an utterly different sphere. We can persuade ourselves that love and sacrifice were all right for him, for he was really God, but that these matters are irrelevant to us as purely human beings.

But if we think of Jesus Christ as having a detailed supernatural foreknowledge of the manner and meaning of his passion, even if we find some basis for this way of thinking in the gospel narrative, are we not coming pretty close to the docetic heresy and are in danger of removing him from our human condition? Indeed, are we not nullifying the significance of the passion itself, if we think of it not as a great moment of history in which great decisions were taken with all the risk that must attend any human decision, but rather as the acting out of a series of events of which the script had already been written in the counsels of God and was known to the chief actor in these events? Is not this to introduce a kind of artificiality into it all?

At the opposite extreme from the traditional belief that Jesus foresaw his passion and resurrection and moved into these events in full awareness is the view of some sceptical historians that he expected nothing of the sort and that it all took him by surprise. Debates over the historical reliability of the gospels have been going on for a long time, but many of the questions still being discussed were raised back in the eighteenth century by one of the earliest and most radical critics of the New Testament, Herbert Reimarus. According to him, Jesus was primarily a Jewish nationalist and political revolutionary. He went up to Jerusalem not to die but to seize control of the capital city. The story of his driving the traders out of the Temple is really the account of how he and his followers attempted the forcible occupation of an important public building, rather in the manner of student radicals in more recent times. But, according to Reimarus, Jesus had overestimated the extent of his support among the people. His movement was not strong enough to overthrow the authorities, his followers melted away, the revolt had collapsed and he found himself arrested and sent for trial. The cry from the cross, 'My God, my God, why hast thou forsaken me?' (Mark 15.34) was a cry of defeat and disillusionment. 'It was then,' says Reimarus, 'clearly not the intention of Jesus to suffer and to die, but to build up a worldly kingdom and to deliver the Israelites from bondage. It was in this that God had forsaken him, it was in this that his hopes had been frustrated.'[11]

If the Christian believer is troubled by the traditional belief that Christ, by some supernatural insight, foresaw the events that were to befall him in Jerusalem, the same believer is not likely to get much comfort when he turns to the interpretations of these events by Reimarus and his more recent counterparts. If the traditional belief presented us with a Jesus who is too superhuman to have much meaning for ordinary mortals, the Jesus whom we find in Reimarus is too mean and deluded a specimen of humanity – all too human, we might say – to have any inspirational power for us. We may wonder if we have jumped from the frying pan into the fire.

Yet, as often happens when a radical critical theory is brought into confrontation with the gospel, faith is not destroyed but we are rather driven to understand matters in a deeper, more fundamental way than was possible for us before the criticism was raised. Christianity, as an historical faith, must be exposed to the risks of historical criticism. The Christian believer, if he has integrity, will face and consider even the most radical criticisms of the gospel history – at least, when they come from reputable and conscientious scholars and are backed up by serious arguments. It is surely very much to the credit of Christian theology and an evidence of its intellectual integrity that in the past two or three centuries the methods of historical criticism have come to be generally accepted among theologians and have been fearlessly applied to the Bible. On the whole, the result of such criticism has not been an erosion of faith. In some matters at least, it has led to a deeper understanding of the meaning of Christian faith than was possible in pre-critical days.

But let us return to this difficult question of how Jesus understood his passion. If there is one thing that historical research has made clear, it is that the gospel stories are compounded of actual reminiscences of events on the one hand together with the early church's theological reflections on these events on the other, and the two strands are inextricably entangled with each other. Events always seem different at the time they are happening than they do when we look back at them later, after a period of reflection. This is surely true of the events recorded in the gospels. When the church came to draw up an account of the events of Christ's passion, it may have been after as long as a generation of reflection upon them, and especially of reflection in the light of Old Testament prophecy. In retrospect, it all seemed so clear as the fulfilment of the purposes of God. It was seen as the unfolding of a divine plan of salvation.

But events which are very clear in retrospect may be extremely obscure in prospect. What Christians believed that they plainly saw after the events had happened and they had had a long time to think about them, may well have been very dark, even to the Lord himself, while these events were going on. We do not know what was in his mind as he went up to Jerusalem. Perhaps he hoped that his teaching would still find acceptance – it is, after all, in our very nature to

57

hope, and Christ as man must have hoped. Perhaps even in the agony in the Garden of Gethsemane, he still entertained the possibility that the cup might pass. Perhaps, as Bultmann has speculated, he hoped that even as he stood in the Temple in Jerusalem, the end of the age would come and God would vindicate his faithful ones. On the other side, he must have been equally aware of the dangers. Jerusalem was the stronghold of his enemies. It had a reputation for killing the prophets. The recent killing of John the Baptist was a warning of what others who spoke out might expect.

What historical criticism does for us in our consideration of these matters is to purge our minds of the last traces of the docetic heresy. It forces us to recognize that Jesus went to Jerusalem and, as it was to turn out, to his death, with a human understanding and with human emotions. In following the sequence of events, we are not looking upon someone who, through supernatural sight, perceives in advance everything that is to come so that he has simply to act out a script that he already knows by heart. Only in retrospect could the events be seen in that way. But as the events take place, we are looking on someone who, as truly human, advances with integrity and obedience to his vocation into events the shape of which is still in large measure hidden from him.

But, one may ask, is this not to deny the voluntary character of Jesus' death and so to deprive it of its significance for faith? By no means. A useful comparison can be made from our own times by considering for a moment the death of Martin Luther King, Christian apostle of social change through non-violent methods. He went to Memphis, Tennessee, with hopes of mediating in a labour dispute in that city. His thoughts were probably more concerned with his future plans than with death when, on a spring evening in 1968, he stood on the balcony of his motel. It was at that moment that he was struck down by an assassin. The world was stunned by surprise, shock and horror. But it was not really surprising. King had lived with the possibility of such a death for a long time. He had accepted that possibility as much as any martyr, though its time, place and manner were unknown. In one sense, the shot was sudden and unforeseen; in another, it had been long anticipated.

It is in some such way that we may understand the situation of our Lord as he went up to the city that was to be the scene of his passion. He had dedicated himself wholly to the vocation laid upon him, and there could be no turning back. He knew well that death might befall him – he had been in serious danger even in Galilee. Yet our Lord's knowledge was a human knowledge and for him as for us, the future had still to unfold itself. The human emotions of hope and uncertainty and the conflict between them must have been present in his mind. The New Testament scholar, Raymond Brown, has expressed the matter well in these words: 'A Jesus who walked through the world knowing exactly what the morrow would bring, knowing with certainty that three days after his death his Father would raise him up, is a Jesus who can arouse our admiration, but still a Jesus far from us. He is a Jesus far from a mankind that can only hope in the future and believe in God's goodness, far from a mankind that must face the supreme uncertainty of death with faith but without knowledge of what is beyond. On the other hand, a Jesus for whom the future was as much a mystery, a dread and a hope as it is for us and yet, at the same time a Jesus who could say "Not my will but yours!" – this is a Jesus who could effectively teach us how to live, for this is a Jesus who would have gone through life's real trials.'[12]

So the critical consideration of the gospel narrative leads us to a deeper understanding of its content. We are made to confront Jesus in his full humanity, and surely this does not diminish his stature but rather enhances it. For this is a humanity that transcends any other that we know, a humanity so open towards the Father that, as we reflect on the events of the passion, we can believe with the early Christians that God was indeed at work here.

The Passion and the Spirit

The passion of Jesus Christ is not only a great human drama. Christians have seen in it the decisive moment when God himself has drawn near and made himself known. When we think of the passion and death of Jesus Christ, we are not primarily recalling the fate of an individual, however inspiring that may be. We are meditating on the mystery of God, for here, we believe, the ultimate reality is revealed at its deepest level. And what we learn about that reality is both shattering and strengthening.

It is shattering because it contradicts all our conventional ideas of God. It is no wonder that the cross is considered an offence. The lonely figure of Jesus Christ, following in the way of the cross, seems not so much the revelation of God as rather the contradiction of everything that has been commonly believed about God. 'Almighty

God' is our usual way of addressing him, and even Christians have tended to think of God as a celestial monarch, disposing of the world according to his sovereign will, untouched and untroubled by the storms that rage below. Some of our hymns of the passion encourage these ideas: 'The Father on his sapphire throne expects his own anointed Son'. This is surely a terrible misunderstanding. The point is that we are being invited to see God in the Son, in this despised, rejected, suffering figure, not to look away from him to some distant sapphire throne, as if the reality were there rather than here, and as if what we see on Calvary is a bad dream obscuring the reality. To think in that way would be to miss the whole meaning of incarnation and passion, which is that God comes among us in weakness and humility to stand with us in the midst of the created order.

Where we go wrong is that we bring along some ready-made idea of God, wherever we may have learned it, and then we try to make Jesus Christ fit in with that idea of God. Of course, I am not denying that there is a 'natural theology' and that all men can have some knowledge of God. But if we take the idea of a revelation of God in Christ seriously, then we must be willing to have our understanding of God corrected and even revolutionized by what we learn in Jesus Christ. In other words, we cannot fit Christ into some previously established theistic understanding of the world. We have to move in the opposite direction, and this means that it is through Christ that we have to understand God and his relation to the world, so far as we can understand those matters. We have to begin with the cross, with what has happened here on earth and in the course of human history, not with the exalted deity on the sapphire throne of pious imagining.

Just because there is some universal knowledge of God, the word 'God' is not a specifically Christian word. There are many gods and many religions. To be sure, something of the true God is known in all religions, for the whole creation has been called into being through his Word. But it is also the case that the knowledge of God is easily perverted, and that man has a tendency to make God in his own image rather than let God be truly God. This means that the God of Christian faith inevitably conflicts with some of the other gods that are revered in the world, to the extent that these gods have been represented as world rulers, as powers and principalities, as national gods or as the supernatural patrons of cultures and institutions, as realities above this world but not involved in its sufferings –

or, more briefly, in any way that does not acknowledge the primacy of love in God. And here it must be said that one is talking not only about non-Christian religions or philosophical ideas of God, for Christians themselves have been only too prone to think of God in distorted and unworthy ways that are not based on the revelation in Christ.

When we consider this almost universal tendency to make power rather than love the defining characteristic of God, it is not surprising when we hear that in the ancient world Christians were ridiculed for worshipping a crucified God – the very idea seemed self-contradictory. Yet, as St Paul tells us, 'although there may be so-called gods in heaven or on earth – as indeed there are many "gods" and many "lords" – yet for us there is one God, the Father, from whom are all things and for whom we exist, and one Lord, Jesus Christ, through whom are all things and through whom we exist' (I Cor. 8.5, 6). We cannot think of God apart from Jesus Christ, and we cannot think of Jesus Christ apart from his passion and death.

Because of the difference of its God from other possible gods, the Christian faith has developed its own language for naming the mystery of God. The word 'God' by itself is too ambiguous and too prone to misunderstanding. Thus Christianity developed its own trinitarian language for speaking of God. God is Father, Son and Holy Spirit. Only some such conception comes anywhere near to being adequate to the God who is known in Christian faith. The triune God is no mere theological speculation, but is the church's attempt to spell out, in however faltering a way, something of the richness and distinctiveness of the specifically Christian experience of God.

So if we would understand the cross and passion of Christ on a deeper level, as revelation of God as well as human drama, we must try to think of these events in relation to the triune God. We shall then see how deeply the cross enters into the understanding of God, Father, Son and Holy Spirit, and that means into our understanding of the deepest reality there is.

In this threefold meditation on the passion in relation to the triune God, it is convenient to think of the persons of the Trinity in the reverse of the usual order, that is to say, we begin with God the Holy Spirit. We do so because the Holy Spirit is God in his nearness to us. The Spirit has proceeded or come forth from the Father into the creation. The Spirit is God, active and present in the whole created order and especially among human beings who are themselves spiritual and capable of responding to the Holy Spirit of God.

We hear much these days of the movement of the Spirit in the church, and of the spread of charismatic and pentecostalist forms of Christianity. Today, as in the past, strange things are sometimes said and done in the name of the Holy Spirit. How do we recognize the genuine work and presence of the Holy Spirit and distinguish it from counterfeits? We can only reply that we cannot think of the Spirit apart from Christ. At his baptism, the Spirit came upon him in fullness, and it is to Christ we must look if we are to learn the quality of a truly spiritual or Spirit-filled life. In that life, the cross and passion have a central place. That is the work of the Spirit which accords with Christ's passion and cross, and which leads into love, patience, peace, long-suffering, true community. If anything that claims to be the work of the Spirit leads in directions away from these or in conflict with these, then we must say that in these cases we are not dealing with the Holy Spirit of God.

Of all the teaching about the Holy Spirit in the New Testament, perhaps the most profound comes from St Paul, and it is very relevant to our theme, for we see the Holy Spirit's activity in a way that links it with the passion of Christ. The Spirit is depicted by Paul as the bringer of life and liberation, and as lifting the whole creation towards God, 'The whole creation has been groaning in travail together but the Spirit is at work in it to set it free "from its bondage to decay"' (Rom. 8.21, 22). The impression we have of the Spirit in this passage may remind us of what some modern philosophers have called the *nisus* of the universe – a creative transforming striving which is always bringing forth the new and is raising the universe to higher levels of being. Admittedly, this is a speculative interpretation of the work of the Spirit on subpersonal levels, though it would seem that there must be some dynamic force at work to account for the evolution of the natural world. But spirit (whether the divine Spirit or the human spirit) is more typically understood in personal terms, and Paul immediately passes to this personal work of the Holy Spirit. 'Not only the creation', he tells us, 'but we ourselves, who have the first fruits of the Spirit, groan inwardly as we wait for adoption as sons . . . Likewise the Spirit helps us in our weakness; for we do not know how to pray as we ought, but the Spirit himself intercedes for us with sighs too deep for words' (Rom. 8.23, 26). The travail of the creation, as it seeks to bring to birth a new order, is continuous with the travail of persons seeking a new relationship with God. But in all this striving and suffering of the created order, it is the Spirit that is at work. He joins in the sighs of longing of the creation, he shares in the struggles and agony of the creatures, he himself is the dynamic power working in their midst to bring the creation nearer to God's loving intentions for it. His sighs and prayers mingle with theirs or, better expressed, their sighs and prayers are but their response to the deeper striving of God the Spirit in them and with them.

From the very beginning, then, the Holy Spirit has been in the creation and among men, sharing their suffering and striving for their liberation – and it is this picture of God the Spirit that gives us a juster understanding of God's nature than the picture of the sapphire throne. It is all of a piece with the cross and passion, for we can see the cross as the culmination in the Spirit-filled man, Jesus Christ, of that costly travail of the divine Spirit for the perfecting of the creation that has gone on through all the ages.

The Spirit is still sighing in our midst. 'Today if you will hear his voice, harden not your hearts' (Ps. 95.8). Our meditation on the passion of Christ points us to the passionate striving of the Spirit. He invites us to a deeper spiritual life, not in the sense of tranquil contemplation of eternal truths, but in the sense of letting our lives be invaded and disturbed by the prayers and longing of the Spirit, yes, by his travail and suffering in and for the whole creation, for that striving of the Spirit is one with the passion of Christ.

The Passion and the Son

Jesus Christ, if I may borrow a phrase of Bishop Robinson, is 'the human face of God'. In him we meet God communicating himself to us in the medium of our own human existence.

To say that Christ is the human face of God is, of course, to assert nothing less than that he *is* God, and at an early stage in the history of the church Christians realized that one cannot worship Christ or attach ultimacy to his teachings or make for him the claims that Christians do make, if he is anything less than God. The oneness of Christ with God was decisively asserted at Nicaea, and with that assertion went the rejection of Arianism and any other form of belief that would make Christ only a creature, even the most exalted of creatures. Theologically, Christ's relation to God found expression in the teaching which identified him with the second person of the Trinity. This second person of the Trinity, in turn, is understood as that mode of the divine being through which God creates an ordered world and relates himself to that world and so to the history and affairs of men.

Two metaphors have been traditionally used for the second person of the Trinity, and these both express the closeness, indeed, the identity of Christ with God. The first metaphor is sonship. We call Jesus Christ the Son of God, and a son is of the very flesh and blood of his father, a distinct being, yet at the same time an extension and continuation of the father's being. The second metaphor is language. We call Christ also the Word of God, and a word is not separable from the person who speaks it and whose mind it brings to expression. Thus to speak of Christ as Son of God or Word of God means that he is one in being or consubstantial with the Father.

But is all this talk not just a lot of nonsense? That a man should be also God sounds so improbable, so absurd, that we can hardly blame reasonable people for thinking that Christianity is, after all, just a gigantic illusion. And especially such a man as Jesus of Nazareth – he seems a very poor candidate. We have very little information about him – though, as Kierkegaard pointed out, even if we had all the historical information the most fastidious scholar could desire, this would not be relevant to the claim of faith that in this man we encounter God himself. The information we have would hardly suggest that here is the human face of God, for what we do know about him shows him rejected by his society and dying a shameful death. Surely, if one were to entertain for a moment the possibility that a man could reveal God, it would not be this man. At the very least, it would have needed an Oxford don (or the equivalent). Of course, people were saying this sort of thing in Jesus' own time: '"Is not this the carpenter's son?" And they were all offended' (Matt. 13.55, 57).

I am not so foolish as to think that one can give some neat explanation of the faith that God was in Christ. Kierkegaard called it the 'absolute paradox'. On the other hand, I cannot feel at ease with those who say that we just have to accept it as a paradox or absurdity that transcends human reason, and leave it at that. To be sure, we accept a great many less exalted absurdities. But we have a duty to be reasonable. This means that we have a duty to understand, as far as we can, the truths of the Christian faith.

But before we reflect further, we have to ask whether we may not be creating difficulties for ourselves. Could it be that the whole notion of God's being present in an obscure Palestinian peasant seems so outrageously absurd because, as so often happens, we are working with a pre-Christian idea of God and thinking of him in terms of power more than of love? If God's normal habitat, so to speak, is a sapphire throne somewhere far off in the empyrean, then it does put a great strain on credulity to be told that one can encounter him on a gibbet outside a fanatical oriental city. But if we take the Christian message seriously and believe that God is primarily love – what then? This would mean that humility and the form of a servant are not disguises of God and not unnatural to him, but of his very essence. And this would mean in turn that he cannot draw near as a prince or even as a professor, but only in some utterly lowly and obscure form. Kierkegaard grasped the essential point here very clearly. If God in his love, he said, is resolved to identify with mankind, he must do so at the level of the humblest and take the form of a servant. 'But this servant-form is no mere outer garment . . . it is his true form and figure. For this is the unfathomable nature of love, that it desires equality with the beloved, not in jest merely, but in earnest and truth.'[13]

There are two ways in which we can explore further the belief that the crucified Christ is the human face of God.

In the first approach, we begin from the consideration of what it means to be a human person. The human being is not a finished, ready-made product. Rather, we have to say that man is searching for his identity and trying to discover a true humanity. He is a creature who is also creative, a finite being who nevertheless has a sense and taste for the infinite. His is an open kind of being, and it is open towards God. Man bears obscurely within himself the image of God, and he moves towards his fulfilment to the extent that he advances along that open road towards God. Christians believe that in Jesus Christ a true humanity did come to light and that in him the image of God was perfectly revealed. But even in him it was not (and by its very nature it could not be) something static and ready made. It had to come to fulfilment in the actual deeds and strivings of his life, and perhaps it was only in those final hours of the passion and cross that the image of God shone out in all its clarity and the perfect union of Christ with the Father came about. For the most godlike thing in Jesus Christ was his creative self-outpouring in love, a self-outpouring like that of the Father from whom all things have their being; and the climax of that self-outpouring of Christ was his passion and death. I am saying that was the climax, but the process had been going on through all his ministry, yes, and before that in the preparation for his ministry. We can again learn at this point from Kierkegaard, who says that it is a mistake to speak only of the last phase of our Lord's life as his passion – the whole life was a passion.

To think of the question from the human side and to see the creative passion of Christ as the manifestation of the divine image in him keeps before us the important truth that Jesus was indeed fully a human being, and it also allows our thinking about him to recapitulate the way of the earliest disciples, who had joined themselves to a man, Jesus of Nazareth, and then at some point, whether sooner or later, became convinced that this man was also the anointed of God. Many New Testament scholars would say that it was only after the sufferings of the cross and the resurrection that the disciples made the identification. Thus Peter, in his Pentecost sermon, could say: 'Let all the house of Israel therefore know assuredly that God has made him both Lord and Christ, this Jesus whom you crucified' (Acts 2.36).

But there is a second approach, a more profound one, and the church soon came to it. It begins not from what one might call the deification of man, but from the humanity of God – even, one might say, the humility of God. What is meant by this? We mean that already in creating man in his own image and in sharing with man something of his own creative and personal being, God was already committing himself to the incarnation, to standing alongside man in the struggles and testing of finite existence. Jesus Christ was not an afterthought on the part of God. If we think of creation as taking place through that outgoing aspect of God's being which we call his Word, the second person of the Trinity, then we can say that already in that eternal Word the suffering Messiah is included. For God was putting something of himself into the creation from the beginning, and eventually he must find perfect expression in the creation. For the creation is no casual production. God cares about it, and especially for those creatures whom he has made capable of communion with himself. Wherever there is caring, there is vulnerability and suffering, or at least the readiness to suffer. Perhaps where there is infinite caring, there is a willingness to bear infinite suffering. The cross and passion are already there in God before the actual historical passion of Jesus of Nazareth. We could therefore only think it incongruous that God should reveal himself in Jesus if we thought of God as other than a God of love. It is not incongruous if the creator is a God of love who in the act of creating committed himself to his creatures and resolved to stand beside them through all the risks and adventures of the creation's unfolding.

We have noted already Kierkegaard's insistence that God's servant-form was no mere disguise but a consequence of his love, and he goes so far in one place to say that God 'has, so to speak, imprisoned himself in his resolve'. He has committed himself irreversibly to his creation, and to the suffering which must attend that commitment. We may also recall some words of Bonhoeffer: 'Man's religiosity makes him look in his distress to the power of God in the world: God is the *deux ex machina*. The Bible directs man to God's powerlessness and suffering; only the suffering God can help.'[14] The witness of another theologian, Moltmann, is similar: 'The suffering and dying of Jesus . . . are works of God towards himself and therefore at the same time passions of God.'[15]

All our popular ideas of God as the power behind the scenes who will ensure that everything will turn out well are shattered by the Christian understanding of God as the one who stands with us in suffering, the eternal Word incarnate in Jesus Christ.

The Passion and the Father

In a number of passages in his writings, Karl Barth indicates that Good Friday is the day of the Father, Easter Day is the day of the Son and Whitsunday is the day of the Holy Spirit. At first sight, this may seem a somewhat surprising allocation of the days – or, at least, of two of them. Would it not be more natural to say that Good Friday is the day of the Son, the day of his suffering and sacrifice, while Easter is the day of the Father, the day when the power of God was manifested in raising the Son from the dead, in frustrating the designs of the evil powers, and in restoring order and hope to the creation? But if we think more deeply about the matter, we shall see that Barth is at least half right – and perhaps theologians are rarely more than half right, certainly never more than two-thirds right!

Good Friday is a day of mystery and darkness. We are told that there was darkness over the land during the hours when Jesus hung upon the cross, and whether or not there was literal darkness on that occasion, there is certainly a metaphysical darkness over Calvary. Why should the man from God and for God be destroyed by his fellow men? Was it not possible for the cup to pass? Was all this the foreordained plan of God, and what kind of a world is it where God plans things this way? These are the questions provoked by the cross, and there is no answer to them. In this metaphysical darkness, as I have called it, even Christ uttered his cry of dereliction. It was certainly not all clear to him.

The Father is the most mysterious and hidden region of the Trinity, and that is the reason for our having left the topic of the passion and the Father to the end, after having considered the passion and the Spirit, and the passion and the Son. The Spirit is God among us, the Son is God in human form, but the Father is the primordial source of being, the abyssal depth of Godhead. It is from him that the Son is begotten and the Spirit proceeds. There must be much in the Father that utterly surpasses our powers of comprehension. We say that he is revealed in the Son, yet we acknowledge that inevitably in the incarnation there is a veiling as well as a revealing, for the infinite is being expressed in the finite. We read in the New Testament that 'God is light, and in him is no darkness at all' (I John 1.5). But when light is concentrated above a certain intensity, it blinds us and appears to us as darkness. There are unknown depths of God which must appear dark to us. Perhaps we can only make a negative statement and say, in some well-chosen words of Michael Ramsey, that in the Father 'there is no un-Christlikeness at all'.[16] There are regions of the Godhead that must be veiled from finite understanding, but the Christian belief is that there is nothing in him that contradicts what has been revealed in his human face, Jesus Christ.

But even to believe in this negative formulation that there is no un-Christlikeness in the primordial source of being is to believe much indeed. It is a belief that makes a great difference to the lives of those who hold it, and which enables them to live in this perplexing world with a hope that they could not otherwise have.

Michael Ramsey was making his point about relating our thought about God to what we have seen in Christ in the course of a discussion in which he claimed that if the concept of God has come to seem incredible to many people nowadays, it may well be due to the fact that our concept of God has not been truly Christianized and that there are un-Christlike elements lurking in it. This has been very much my contention too in these meditations. As Christians, we have to think of the Father in the light of Jesus Christ, and not least from the suffering of Christ.

When we ask how the passion and cross of Christ affect our understanding of the Father, then we can rule out some mistaken ideas right away. We cannot think, for instance, of the Father as a stern judge, exacting the death of the Son as a penalty for sin, though many Christians have in fact thought in that way. We cannot think either, I would say, of the Father remote and secure on his sapphire throne, himself untouched by the passion of the Son.

Am I saying then that the Father, too, God in the very depth of his Godhood, is touched and affected by the passion? That is surely what we must say, if we are determined to know God through Jesus Christ, and not in some other way of our own choosing, whether it comes from Greek philosophy or modern philosophy, from Platonism or the Enlightenment, from natural theology or deism, or any other such source.

But, then, does not this conflict with the church's teaching about the impassibility of God, the doctrine that God cannot suffer and is without passions? No doubt it does, if that doctrine is taken to imply a frozen God, 'apathetic' and not able to be affected. But surely there would be something un-Christlike in such a God. A God of love is inevitably vulnerable, for there is no love that does not suffer.

I think, however, that the doctrine of the divine impassibility can be understood in a different way – a way which is more Christian. I would prefer to call it the 'serenity' of God, and by that I mean that to God there belongs a deep serenity that can never be overwhelmed, so that he is able to accept and to absorb and even to transmute into good all the sufferings of his creatures. It is not that he is untouched by these sufferings, but that he has the power and capacity to take them on himself and not be destroyed by them. In this sense we might say that God is impassible, and certainly we acknowledge the contrast between his serenity and the way in which we ourselves can be so easily overwhelmed, discouraged, sometimes hardened and embittered, by suffering and frustration. But such serenity or impassibility as we may ascribe to God have nothing to do with apathy or immunity from pain. More typical of God than any impassibility are his love, his care and his concern. These surely lay him open to grief and vexation, but he has an infinite capacity to bear them.

Sometimes we meet Christians who absorb the suffering of others and even give their lives in such ministry. Eusebius, in his history of the early church, mentions the ministry of healing and comforting that went on during an outbreak of pestilence, and he says: 'Many also, who had healed and strengthened others, themselves died, transferring the death of the others upon themselves.' I had once a colleague with whom I was serving in an institution deeply divided by feuds and factions. He was tireless in his work of reconciliation, absorbing the strains into himself, until that costly atoning ministry brought him to a premature death. Such cases give us a glimpse of God's dealing with pain and suffering. But the difference is that his capacity for absorption and transmutation is infinite.

It is highly significant that in specifically Christian God-language, that is to say, in trinitarian language, we call the deepest, most ultimate region of Godhead, the Father. So when we speak of the eternal Father, we mean that from the very beginning the divine reality has stood in a loving relationship to something or someone other than himself. There never was a time, so to speak, when God was a lonely eremite or a self-contained absolute, as he has been represented in some philosophies. There never was a time, the early church declared, as against the Arians, when the Son was not. From eternity there has been a loving relation, and we may not think of God without it. It is not something that has come about subsequently. It belongs to the very nature of God, in Christian belief.

Through the Son, there takes place creation, and perhaps this too has been an eternal activity on God's part, for the Christian doctrine of creation teaches the God-dependent status of the world, not necessarily that it had a beginning in time. When we bring the creation into consideration, we see that God's fatherhood is extended to the creatures, at least, to those creatures who are capable of responding as children. 'Doubtless, thou art our Father,' says an Old Testament prophet in a passage which speaks of God's mercy, compassion and yearning towards his people (Isa. 63.7–16). It certainly would be hard to square this passage with the belief that God cannot feel or suffer anything. It even contains the words, 'in all their affliction, he was afflicted', and although this translation is not universally accepted, it does represent a great theological insight. How indeed could God be a Father, and not be afflicted in the afflictions of his children?

In the New Testament, Jesus teaches the disciples to pray to God as their Father. He himself conceives his relation to God in filial terms, and in a more general way the New Testament can speak of God as the 'Father of spirits' and of human beings as potentially his sons and daughters.

This, then, is the root of Godhood, the first person of the Trinity, God in his most ultimate divinity. He is no self-centred absolute, no unmoved and unmovable mover, no unfeeling impersonal principle, not even a lonely monarch distantly presiding over the universe, but a Father yearning for his creatures, a Father who is most fully revealed in the suffering crucified Saviour. And the fact that he too can be touched and affected certainly does not make him any less God or any less adorable, but rather more so. The God of Christian faith, we could say, is great enough to be humble.

At the beginning of this meditation, I said that theologians are usually only half right, or at most two-thirds right, and perhaps I should now confess that in this meditation and in the two that have preceded it I have dwelt mainly on one half of the truth about God – the truth of his nearness, his loving concern, his sharing in the suffering of the creation, the truth, in short, that is set forth in the passion of Jesus Christ. There is certainly an excuse for dwelling on this side of the truth, for it is so often obscured by wrong ideas of God's majesty, impassibility, sovereignty and the like. But of course, there is more to be said – and there always is, when we speak of the inexhaustible content of Christian faith. One would have to speak also of God's ultimacy and transcendence, and these are also essential to his Godhead. In that sense, one would have to say that Easter Day as well as Good Friday is the day of the Father. But we would have to understand this in a way which did not in the least contradict what we have learned from the cross and passion. It is not as if on Easter Day God annuls or abolishes or simply reverses what happened on Good Friday by an exercise of almighty power. It is rather that by the ultimate power of his love, he is able to take up all the suffering and poignancy of the passion and bring out of it something new and renewing, the event we call resurrection.

But that would be another story. For the present we are thinking of the passion, and it is enough to contemplate the love of the God who has drawn near in that event.

5

THE OVERCOMING

Resurrection is not the cancelling out of the cross, for there is no way to resurrection except through the cross. Indeed, one might even say that resurrection is the freedom born of the cross. St Paul prayed 'that I might know him and the power of his resurrection, and may share his sufferings, becoming like him in his death, that if possible I may attain the resurrection from the dead' (Phil. 3.10–11). So I have rather carefully chosen for this section of the book the title 'The Overcoming', rather than some such misleading expression as 'The Triumph' or 'The Victory'. For 'overcoming' stresses the continuity with what has gone before, the perfecting of the same work. The Overcoming is continuous with the Coming and carries through to their culmination the Sharing, the Coming, the Teaching, the Passion. The drama of God's humble concern for his creation is all of one piece.

Resurrection

There is nothing more central to Christian faith and to Christian proclamation than resurrection – first, the resurrection of Jesus Christ, and then the promised resurrection of the dead. Most scholars are agreed that the church would never have come into existence and there never would have been a Christian movement if the first disciples had not believed beyond doubt that Jesus Christ had risen from the dead and was alive among them. Paul says frankly: 'If Christ has not been raised, then our preaching is in vain and your faith is in vain!' (I Cor. 15.14). This, by the way, looks like a possible answer to those modern philosophers who ask, 'What would falsify

Christian faith?' The point of their question is that if the Christian cannot specify a state of affairs that would be incompatible with the truth of Christianity so that his faith is compatible with any state of affairs whatever, then that faith must be something so vague, amorphous and incoherent that it can neither be rightly believed nor disbelieved. But here Paul seems to be putting faith on the line, so to speak. It stands or falls with the resurrection of Jesus Christ. If Christ has not been raised, then Christian faith and preaching are revealed as false. It is all an illusion.

We may think that Paul has chosen a singularly weak and vulnerable article on which to make the whole faith depend. The resurrection is surely just about the most incredible item in the Christian faith. Dead men do not rise – surely we all know that. To say that Christian faith depends on the truth of the resurrection of Christ is to offer an unbearable offence to the modern mind. Incidentally, it seems to have been an offence to the ancient mind too, for when Paul preached on the resurrection at Athens, the people laughed at him. They knew as well as people today that dead men do not rise.

Would it not therefore have been much safer and simpler if Paul had said that Christianity stands or falls by the beauty of Christ's teaching or the integrity of his character or something else that is acceptable to the liberal secularized mind? But here we strike on a strange fact, which was made very clear by Kierkegaard in the aftermath of the Enlightenment. The strange fact is this, that the passion with which men and women commit themselves to Christianity (or, on the other hand, turn away from it) seems to be proportionate to the element of offence and paradox in it. On the other hand, if it is all explained and made acceptable, if Christianity is simply the republication of natural religion so that it is at bottom no more than what reasonable men have believed since the beginning of civilization, then it is deprived of interest, and is no longer anything to get excited or passionate about. Resurrection (and the same can be said about incarnation) may be something very difficult to believe, but at least one can say, to believe or not to believe is of the highest importance. If Jesus Christ is the incarnate Word and the risen Lord, he is infinitely more exciting than if he is simply another in the long line of religious teachers, the Rabbi of Nazareth, 'historically so difficult to get information about', as Karl Barth once said, 'and when it is got, one whose activity is so easily a little commonplace alongside more than one other founder of a religion and even alongside many later representatives of his own religion'.

But is resurrection totally incredible? It may be true that the interest and passion of Christian faith depend on elements of novelty, paradox, even offence in it, but we are not being asked to believe nonsense or to give up our rationality. We are being asked to think more deeply. To say that Christian faith stands or falls with the resurrection of Jesus Christ from the dead is not so simple and straightforward an assertion as it appears at first sight. What is resurrection? When we read Paul's own further remarks on the subject, we soon realize that resurrection is a very subtle idea indeed. It is certainly nothing so naive as the raising of a natural body, that is to say, the resuscitation of a corpse. Resurrection is not some clearly definable concept (and the same can be said about incarnation) but an image, a symbol, a mythological idea, if you like, pointing to something which lies at the very limits of our understanding.

But if I am now saying that the idea of resurrection is a somewhat obscure one, does that not have repercussions on what was said earlier? If we cannot say with at least some clarity what we mean by resurrection, then we are back to the beginning. The bold specification of an article by which Christian faith stands or falls, the acknowledgment that such and such a state of affairs would falsify faith, may not be so bold after all, if that all-important state of affairs is left so vague that no one could recognize it or judge whether or not it obtained. So let us see if we can clear our minds on what we mean by belief in the resurrection of Christ. We have already agreed that we are dealing with an evocative image rather than a precise concept, but we have to ask what it is that the image brings to expression.

We might begin by recalling an expression used by William James. He talked about the 'cash value' of an idea. By that he meant the difference that it makes in our experience and what it contributes to our conduct of life. Now it is surely not difficult to point to the 'cash value' of belief in the resurrection. For the first disciples, it made all the difference in the world in their experience and conduct. It transformed them from a bewildered group of men and women mourning a dead leader and a lost cause to the most explosive revolutionary movement the world has ever known. Resurrection for them was something they were already experiencing in themselves – a new quality of life filled with energy, love, joy, hope for the future. Becoming a Christian was already to share in resurrection, to be made a new creature. Paul interpreted baptism as a dying with

74

Christ, a burying of the old life, and a rising with Christ into a new life. In this sense, Christians have never ceased down to the present day to know the meaning of resurrection, both in their own lives and in that of the Christian community. And this is no mere metaphor. It is the cash value of the idea, the present empirical reference, as distinct from what resurrection might mean as a report about the past or an expectation for the future. To recognize this is an important step towards specifying what is meant by resurrection. Wherever the gospel has been preached in two thousand years, a profound transformation of human life has taken place and we may fairly call it 'resurrection' – a radical renewal in which people have risen from the death of sin and apathy to a new quality of life that is in every way more truly human, personal and spiritual.

Some scholars have claimed that the resurrection of Christ is simply to be identified with the life of the new Christian community, so that we need look no further. Jesus dies, but there arose the Christian church which is his body and which extends to all generations the incarnation of his spirit. This of course, is true and important. But surely more is meant by the resurrection of the Lord than just that the church arose in the place of its dead leader and continued what he had begun. The early church did not generate its resurrection life out of its own resources or even out of its nostalgic memories of a lost teacher. It came to life because there was already there a life prior to its own. It knew in its midst a living Lord – a Lord who lived not only in them but in himself. Many people, I suppose, can be said to live on for a time after their deaths in their children and in their friends, because their memory still influences these people. But the case of Jesus is different. He did not survive as a gradually fading memory and influence in the hearts of his followers, but as the very source of their new life. He had opened up that new life for them and was himself the firstfruits of the resurrection. The disciples came to believe in the risen Lord in various ways. Some, like Paul himself, had visions and encounters, others, less dramatically but none the less surely, knew his presence in the prayers, in the fellowship, in the breaking of bread. And again this is something that has persisted in the church.

For people still claim to know Christ's living presence. Bishop Arthur Vogel has written a little book which he has called *The Power of his Resurrection*.[17] The expression comes, of course, from a prayer in one of Paul's letters: 'That I may know him and the power of his

75

resurrection' (Phil. 3.10). Bishop Vogel subtitled his book, 'The Mystical Life of Christians'. We must not be put off by the use of the word 'mystical' here. It is not something very esoteric that is meant, but simply a relation to Christ as a living person. To be 'in Christ', says the bishop, is like being in your own home, enjoying the personal presence of your loved one, the presence that supports you and makes you the person you are. Belief that Christ lives on is no theoretical belief but the knowledge of his continuing presence. Many have testified to this presence, and if indeed there is a God who cares for his creatures, would we not expect that Christ would live on in God?

This brings us to a last point about resurrection. Paul, like other New Testament writers, says that it was God who raised up Christ. What does it mean to say that God is in these events? We do not mean that from outside God intervened to cancel out the death of Christ by the miracle of resurrection. We mean rather that God was truly on the inside of these events. In Christ he took upon himself the evil and suffering of the world, but he is able to absorb and transform it all and to open the new way forward that we call resurrection. This means too that Christ was no anomaly, no highly exceptional individual briefly flickering in the wastes of history, but the clue to what God is about in history. The resurrection of Christ is the pointer to the final resurrection of the dead, the overcoming by God of all that stands in the way of the perfecting of his creation.

Ascension

For the last time the disciples have seen Jesus face to face. He has promised them that they will receive power from the Holy Spirit, and he has charged them to be his witnesses, first in Jerusalem, then in all Judaea and Samaria, and finally beyond that to the uttermost parts of the earth. And then, we are told, 'he was taken up; and a cloud received him out of their sight' (Acts 1.9).

We call this event the ascension. The story comes, of course, from an age in which men's conceptions of the universe were very different from those that are current today. Some people in the first century were still flat-earthers. They thought in terms of the old Babylonian cosmology, in which the earth was supposed to be a flat expanse overarched by the firmament of the sky, with heaven above and hell below. Some people, however, were familiar with the much more up-to-date Ptolemaic cosmology, according to which the earth was supposed to lie at the centre of a number of concentric crystalline spheres which carried the various heavenly bodies. But whether one held to the older or the newer fashion of thought, heaven was thought to be 'up there'. Beyond the sky and the visible heavenly bodies lay a numinous region, believed to be the abode of God or the gods. Thus, to go to be with God meant to rise from this earth into the heavenly places above, and the idea of the divine presence had traditionally been symbolized among the Hebrews by a cloud.

It was, so to speak, quite a cosy world which the ancients visualized – a world not too vast in extent, and one which had existed for a few thousand years at the most. Men could feel at home in such a world, they could believe themselves pretty near to the centre of things, and so they could also believe that they counted for something in the universe. It all seemed to have been providentially designed for their benefit. But the rise of modern science has shattered that comfortable picture of the universe. Probably man in all his history has never undergone a more traumatic experience than the Copernican revolution which dethroned him from the centre of things. That experience in the history of the race might be likened to the traumatic experience of which psychoanalysts have made so much in tracing the history of the individual – expulsion from the security of the womb into a vast, cold, uncertain and alien world.

In modern times, man has come to realize that his earth is a mere speck in the immensity of space, his history a fleeting moment in the eons of time. Some famous words in Pascal's *Pensées* express the new feeling of loneliness and terror that was beginning to grip men's minds in the time of the rise of science: 'The eternal silence of these infinite spaces fills me with dread.'[18] In modern times, poets, philosophers and novelists have expressed man's sense of lostness and disorientation in the trackless expanses of space-time. It can be summed up in Nietzsche's words: 'The centre is everywhere.' The once familiar contours have disappeared, the gods have withdrawn. No matter how far one might ascend into the heavens, one would find not the glories of the heavenly abode but just the silent spaces, just nothing. It was not news when a Russian cosmonaut naively reported that he had seen no angels during his trip aloft.

If then our conception of the universe has changed so entirely, does it still make sense for Christians to affirm of Christ in the creed that 'he ascended into heaven'? Admittedly, the scientific revolution

77

has once and for all destroyed the mythological picture of the cosy, familiar, earth-centred universe, and ascension in any literal sense is an idea which we would find it impossible to believe – indeed, we could scarcely make sense of it. But the point of the story lay elsewhere. Using the mythological imagery with which they were familiar in their own culture, the disciples expressed in the story of the ascension a tremendous claim for Jesus Christ – a cosmic claim, as we might say. They had known him face to face, a particular man who lived at a particular time in a particular corner of the world. But they had come to perceive in him something of universal and all-compelling significance. The life-span of this particular human being, Jesus of Nazareth, was now over and had vanished into the past, as all human life-spans do. His physical presence was no longer available. But that universal significance and influence that the disciples had seen in him had not vanished. On the contrary, it was set free from the limitations of his particular historical existence in a tiny corner of space and time, so that the living and vivifying presence of Christ would thenceforth be available at all times and in all places. Yes, available even in this very different and somewhat terrifying universe, which these men of ancient times did not foresee. For Christian faith in the ascended Lord means for us today that even among the vast silent spaces of this universe, the personal reality that came to expression in Jesus Christ gives us a deeper clue to the meaning of it all than the wheeling galaxies and gas clouds.

It is significant that Christian devotion has claimed that the ascended Lord still bears the marks of the wounds inflicted in his passion. The ascension is not a triumphalist reversal of the passion, but testifies that it is precisely the humble, self-emptying, suffering love of Christ that can overcome the world and point us to the deepest reality of all.

Perhaps too the most recent advances of physical science are more easily reconciled than was the science of the nineteenth century with the belief that personal being, and therefore the highest reach of personal being that we see in Christ, is the clue to the cosmic process. For if modern science has rendered obsolete and incredible the mythological universe assumed by those who produced the ascension story, it seems to have rendered equally obsolete the kind of mechanistic and materialistic view of the universe that even a few decades ago was supposed to be scientifically based. Pascal and his contemporaries were fascinated by the very large and the very small, and contemporary science seems to show that at both extremes the universe runs out into an apparently inexhaustible mystery and complexity. American physicist Harold Schilling writes: 'The more we learn about [nature], the less we need fear it, and the more we can trust it and enter with joyous expectancy into its life and further development.'[19]

The ascension then means that the love of Christ has overcome. It is stronger than any other power and is exalted over all other powers. It is our clue to the mystery of God and to the creative force that sustains the world. In this sense Christ is a present cosmic reality. It is as such a present reality that we must think of Jesus Christ. Our business is not to recall in nostalgic longing a historical figure who inevitably recedes more and more into the past and the details of whose life are of necessity obscure and uncertain. Rather, our business, like that of the first disciples, is to respond to the new vision that Christ has opened up, the vision of a new humanity and even of a new heaven and a new earth. That is a vision that can be realized only if his disciples, now as then, are willing to be his witnesses to the ends of the earth.

Can we say more about this transformation through which the particular historical figure of Palestine becomes the universal ascended Lord? Idealist philosophers have sometimes understood it in far too abstract a way, as if all that happened was that some timeless truths or generalizations were derived from the historical existence and teaching of Jesus Christ and then passed on as a moral and spiritual ideal for later generations. Edward Caird, for instance, after saying that any great idea needs first to be shown in a particular example if it is to gain a hold on the human mind, went on to say that 'we may detach the idea from accidents of space and time and circumstances, and present it as a general principle'. No doubt this is true so far as it goes, but it falls far short of what Christians mean when they speak of the ascension of Christ. Assuredly, the ascension did not turn him into a general principle. He remained, as he had been, a living person, but now alive in God and no longer bounded by the particularities of a human existence in space and time.

This means that the ascension cannot be understood apart from Christ's promise of the Holy Spirit. Indeed, in the New Testament there would appear to be no clear distinction between the spirit of the risen Christ and the Holy Spirit. The Holy Spirit is a parallel figure to Jesus, continuing and making present in every age Jesus' own work. It is through the Spirit that Jesus continues to lead his church, not as an abstract ideal or a noble exemplar or a general metaphysical principle, but as a presence both living and making alive. Jesus Christ is neither a distant figure of past history nor a distant ideal of moral aspiration, but the universal Lord who calls us today into his company and service.

The Life of the Spirit

For a long time in my teaching and writing I tried to avoid using the word 'spirit'. I took this course because of the demands of intellectual honesty, for I think that we should not use words unless we can say with some degree of clearness what we mean by them. Of course, I do not mean that one has got to be able to give a precise and exhaustive definition. There will always be something mysterious about spirit, and the very word is itself originally a metaphor – the breath or the breeze – which people used to name an elusive reality of which they had become aware. But certainly if one is using a word, one ought to be able to give some indication of its meaning. Very often, spirit is misunderstood. It is taken to be a 'ghost in the machine', some subtle essence which inhabits the body but is of a different substance from the body. So because of the difficulty of saying what 'spirit' means, together with the fact that it is often misunderstood, I thought it desirable to leave the word alone.

Yet the word 'spirit' seems to be so much a part of the Christian vocabulary that we can hardly do without it if we would speak adequately of the Christian faith and life. In Christian teaching, spirit is both within and without. Spirit is in man as his deepest and truest self; but spirit is also around man as a divine influence that touches his life. Man is spirit, but God too is spirit, and spirit is thus the mysterious bond that links man and God. In creation, God bestowed a share of spirit upon man. To be sure, man's spiritual nature is often obscured and distorted. Yet so long as there is a recognizably human experience and man has not become a machine or anything merely subhuman, the lineaments of spirit can be discerned.

The first step towards understanding the meaning of 'spirit' is to recognize that this word is more of a verb than a noun. It is not some subtle substance, but a way of acting and behaving. It is his power to act and behave in certain ways that distinguishes the human being as the bearer of spirit and in that respect different from all the other creatures upon earth.

What then is this distinctive kind of behaviour that we call spirit? Could we say that it is man's capacity to go out of himself and beyond himself and above himself? Man is not shut up in himself like a stone or a plant, he is not even bound to instinctive patterns of behaviour like an animal. He goes out from himself in a great many ways, extending himself beyond himself. This happens in his pursuit of knowledge, in his acceptance of responsibility, in his quest of the good, in his creation of beauty in the work of art, in the outreach of love, in the building of community, in the communion of the soul with God, and in whatever else belongs to the richness of the life of the spirit.

And here we strike on a fundamental paradox of human life. The more a human being goes out from himself or beyond himself, the more his spirit is deepened and strengthened, the more he becomes truly a man and a person, the more he grows in likeness to God who is also spirit. On the other hand, the more a human being turns inwards and encloses himself in self-interest, the more he lets himself, in Luther's language, become incurved upon himself, then the less spiritual and the less human he becomes. Indeed, he comes to resemble just another item in the natural world. He becomes 'wooden', shall we say, or like a stone. We remember the words of the gospel: 'Whoever would save his life will lose it; and whoever loses his life for my sake and the gospel's will save it' (Mark 8.35). Human life attains its fullness by pouring itself out.

We see this truth above all in Jesus Christ. He is the truly spiritual man, indeed, he is the one on whom the Spirit of God descended in fullness to dwell with him, so that the Spirit of God and the spirit of Jesus are scarcely to be distinguished. But Jesus is also the one who was constantly going out from himself to others, teaching, healing, forgiving, reconciling and finally humbling himself to the way of the cross. Yet finally, this same Jesus who poured himself out to the uttermost is also the one who manifests the stature of a mature humanity and provides the measure of a fully human and personal life.

Such then is the meaning of spirit on the human level; it is the activity of going out. But God too is Spirit (John 4.24). Must we not say then, on the analogy of spirit as we know it in human life, that 'God is Spirit' means that in a supreme degree, beyond anything we can imagine, God is the One who goes out from himself? He is the self-emptying God. He too must be described in verbs rather than nouns, for he is sharing, coming, even suffering, then overcoming. It is surely significant that in the Nicene Creed the language we use about the Holy Spirit is precisely the language of 'proceeding', that is to say, 'going out'. This in turn goes back to the language of the New Testament where we read that he is 'the Spirit of truth who proceeds from the Father' (John 15.26).

Thus to say that God is Spirit is to say that it belongs to his very nature to pour himself out, even to empty himself. If the Christian revelation is true, God is no proud ruler but the servant in love and humility of his creation. Power alone would never make him God. What makes him God and demands for him our adoration is that he went out of himself in creation, and shared the gift of being with his creatures. He has continued to go forth from himself throughout the history of the creation. In Jesus Christ, we believe, he came forth from his transcendence in a new and decisive way. In the Spirit, he still comes forth to us and draws us into the life of the spirit.

But this life of the spirit does not come easily to us. There seems to operate in human life a kind of force of gravity, to use Simone Weil's metaphor, a downward pull that holds us back from the adventure of spirit. And here we come to the problem of spirituality. By spirituality is meant the process of learning or discipline or discipleship by which we learn the life of the spirit. Spirituality is not, as many people seem to think, an introspective concern with one's own inner health. That would be a distortion, and dangerously close to the becoming incurved upon oneself which is the very opposite of the life of the spirit. This life is one of going out in freedom, love and community. But the pull of gravity seems to be all the other way, shutting us up in sloth, inertia and self-centredness. The church, as the community of the Spirit, should be the training ground where the defensive walls that we build around ourselves are broken down and we are set free really to be ourselves – and that means, to share in the freedom of Christ and so in the very life of God.

Consummation

Christians believe that the human race has not had to struggle alone during the millennia of its history. God has been man's companion since the beginning. God's part in the story has been a constant self-giving. He gave himself in creation itself, he continued to give himself in covenants and promises, he stood beside his people and placed himself at their disposal in the incarnation and passion, he continues to pour out his Spirit. We have been thinking in these meditations chiefly of God in his nearness and companionship, in his waiting upon his creatures and in the humility of his love.

It has been right to stress these aspects of God, for they are distinctively Christian and we cannot miss them if we are determined to know God through his revelation in Jesus Christ. But they are often forgotten, even among Christians, and we revert to pre-Christian ways of thinking of God, wherever they may have come from.

Yet to stress God's nearness and humility cannot mean to deny his transcendence and ultimacy, for these also are essential to the Christian understanding of God. But they are understood in a new way. God's transcendence and ultimacy do not mean that he is untouched by the conflicts of the creation, but that he has an infinite capacity for taking them up into himself, absorbing the evil in them and bringing about a new transformed state of affairs in which there is healing and reconciliation.

To hold such beliefs is also to believe that history has a direction and a goal. God has the capacity to bring his creation to the perfection which he intends for it. He does this not through an arbitrary exercise of power but through his own participation in the creation. The process by which it will come to the goal may be a long one and even a roundabout one, but that the goal will be attained is part of Christian faith, indeed, part of biblical faith, for an eschatological hope is attested in the Old Testament as well as in the New.

That hope is symbolized in a variety of pictorial expressions. It is called the kingdom of heaven, the resurrection of the dead, the second coming of Christ. These are images, not precise concepts. They convey hints and allusions, not descriptive information. The object of any hope can only be partly known so long as the hope remains unfulfilled, and the object of this ultimate or total hope for the whole creation must be hidden from us. Yet it would be impossible to entertain a hope if we had no idea at all of its object. So these images do give to the hope some substance. The kingdom of heaven suggests a state of affairs in which everything will be as God intended, with all the potentialities for good fulfilled. The resurrection of the dead implies that those who have suffered and struggled in the past will participate in the coming peace. Christ's second coming (though the expectation may have originated through a misunderstanding on the part of the disciples) looks for a new manifestation of Christ in which the ambiguities of his first coming will be resolved. But these are no more than pointers to a fulfilment which surpasses the power of imagination.

But can we then believe in such a consummation, if our present understanding of it is so limited? I do not think that our belief depends on our capacity to describe in detail the object of eschatological hope or to construct an intelligible concept of resurrection or to give a convincing demonstration that there is an eternal destiny for the human race. If it can be shown that these things are at least possible and not absurd or self-contradictory, then this is always something. But the basis of the belief is that whole experience of God of which we have set out some few fragments in the foregoing meditations. The God who has shared and suffered and overcome in and with his creation will not allow it to be done away but will fulfil in it his purposes of love.

NOTES

NOTES

1. G. E. Lessing, 'The Education of the Human Race', in *Lessing's Theological Writings*, ed. H. Chadwick, A. & C. Black 1956, p. 96.

2. Thomas Kuhn, *The Structure of Scientific Revolutions*, University of Chicago Press 1962.

3. C. H. Dodd, *The Founder of Christianity*, Macmillan Company, New York 1970, Collins 1971; Fontana edition 1973, p. 26.

4. Martin Luther, in *The Book of Concord*, tr. T. G. Tappert, Fortress Press 1959, p. 365.

5. Jürgen Moltmann, *The Crucified God*, Harper & Row and SCM Press 1974, p. 127.

6. Sir James Frazer, *The Golden Bough*, 3rd edition, vol. IX, *The Scapegoat*, Macmillan 1913, pp. 72ff.

7. F. Nietzsche, 'Of Apostates', *Thus Spake Zarathustra* (1883–92), Everyman Edition 1933, p. 162.

8. Iris Murdoch, *The Sovereignty of the Good*, Routledge & Kegan Paul 1970, especially pp. 34ff.

9. Athanasius, *De Incarnatione*, 25; Mowbrays 1963 edition, p. 55.

10. James Deotis Roberts, *Liberation and Reconciliation*, Westminster Press 1971, pp. 191 and 10.

11. H. Reimarus, 'Concerning the Intention of Jesus' in *Fragments*, Fortress Press 1970 and SCM Press 1971, p. 150.

12. R. E. Brown, *Jesus, God and Man*, Geoffrey Chapman 1968, pp. 104f.

13. S. Kierkegaard, *Philosophical Fragments*, Princeton University Press 1936, pp. 24f.

14. Dietrich Bonhoeffer in a letter to Bethge 16 July 1944, *Letters and Papers from Prison*, revised and enlarged edition, Macmillan Company and SCM Press 1971, p. 361.

15. Moltmann, *The Crucified God*, p. 193.

16. A. M. Ramsey, *God, Christ and the World*, SCM Press 1969, p. 98.

17. A. A. Vogel, *The Power of His Resurrection* (Crossroad Books), Seabury Press 1976.

18. B. Pascal, *Pensées,* ed. L. Lafuma, Editions Delmas, Paris 1952, No. 352; Everyman Edition 1932, No. 206, p. 61.

19. H. K. Schilling, *The New Conciousness in Science and Religion,* United Church Press and SCM Press 1973, p. 225.